THE MASS

Four Encounters with Jesus that will Change Your Life

DR. TOM CURRAN

MCF PRESS

Cover Design by John Anderson

Cover Photograph by Anna Henry

Painting of the face of Jesus appearing on the cover
by Tracy L. Christianson

Library of Congress Number: 2008941012

ISBN 0-9817145-0-1

ISBN 978-09817145-0-9

CONTENTS

Acknowledgements

I gratefully acknowledge the many hands that supported the writing of this book. Most important among them are Lori Georgeson, Tracey Rockwell and Mark Shea, who each played distinctive and significant roles in helping this book make it to print. The scope and significance of Lori's decade-long collaboration with me on this project and so many others would be difficult to overstate. Tracey's efforts to lead the book project and help me make the final lap around the track deserve special mention; she has needed the strength of Samson and the patience of Job. I am grateful to John Anderson's hard work and responsiveness to get us a cover design we really love, and also to Josh Sniffen for his incisive comments and help on several aspects of the book project.

My last acknowledgement goes to my wife Kari and my seven kids for all they underwent on behalf of my finishing this book. I dedicate this book to all of you. Mary Grace, Anne Marie, Mary Catherine, Arianna, John Mark, John Luke and Annelise: you are my delight. Kari, you amaze me. Thanks for your incredible support through all the changing deadlines and sacrifices I asked from you in the name of getting this book done. It finally is. *Thanks be to God.*

IS MASS BORING OR ARE WE?

Being Christian
is not the result of an ethical choice
or a lofty idea,
but the encounter with an event,
a person [Jesus Christ]
which gives life a
new horizon and decisive direction.
Pope Benedict XVI, God is Love

I love going to Mass. But I often hear, "Mass is boring. We say the same thing every Sunday; it doesn't make sense. Why should I go to Mass when I don't get anything out of it?" If you've ever found yourself saying these things or wondering what to say to someone who does, then please keep reading.

Do you go to Mass because you are supposed to but don't really understand what's going on? Do you have a hard time keeping your mind from wandering? Would you like the Mass to have a bigger impact on your life but you're not sure what to do about it? I wrote this book for you. Simply put, the Mass is not dull. We are dull. I know this first hand.

For years my mind was dulled by a lack of awareness. I didn't comprehend what was *really happening* at Mass, what was being *offered to me* and what was being *asked of me*. Too often I sat in the pew watching the priest like an uninterested spectator observing and occasionally reacting to what was happening on the field. Once I realized that the pew was part of the playing field, Mass became a lot less boring. At Mass, there are no seats for spectators. If you are there, even in a pew, you are in the game. Just as a football team is made up of players with different but uniquely important roles, at Mass you and I have a role to play that is irreplaceable and vital. We shouldn't settle for being mere *spectators*. Gradually, I came to see that there is a lot at stake in playing my part well, in being what the Church calls a "full, conscious and active" *participant* at Mass.

When a football team is losing and down to its last play, the quarterback will try to snatch victory from the jaws of defeat by throwing a "Hail Mary" pass. I imagine him in the huddle looking his receivers in the eyes and saying, "This is our last chance. I am counting on you." There is a lot at stake for these receivers. The outcome of the game is being placed in their hands. As dramatic as is that moment in a football game, it pales in comparison to what is at stake when we are "receivers" at Mass. What is placed in our hands is immeasurably more precious than a football, because it is not a *what*, but a *Who:* Jesus Christ. He is counting on you.

FOUR ENCOUNTERS WITH JESUS THAT WILL CHANGE YOUR LIFE

The Catholic Church teaches that Jesus Christ is present at Mass in four distinct ways: in the *community* gathered, in the *Word* proclaimed, in the *priest* who presides, and in the *Eucharist*. But He is not only present, He is active. In fact, the root meaning of the Latin word for "presence" is "to turn towards." Jesus Christ is present at Mass in these four ways, turned towards you, addressing you. Jesus Christ doesn't see a crowd at Mass. He sees you. He intends to come close to you, speak to you, live in you and change your life. As I became more aware of this, a sense of expectation and even drama grew in me. Will I recognize Jesus Christ turning toward me at Mass today? Once I knew that life-changing encounters with Jesus Christ awaited me at every Mass, I began to look and listen for Him with new eyes and ears. It was so much easier to pay attention when I realized what was at stake: missing out on meeting the living Lord, Jesus Christ.

You might be saying to yourself, "I have gone to Mass my whole life and have rarely, if ever, experienced a life-changing encounter with Jesus." That's why I wrote this book. In it, I invite you to take a closer look at what you say and do during Mass. If you are like me and thousands of others who have discovered the message of this book, you will be amazed at what you've been missing.

Chapter by chapter, I accompany you from the time you pull into the church parking lot to the moment you walk out after the final blessing. If I do my job well, you will learn how to recognize and respond to Jesus Christ's drawing near you at Mass. That's my goal: to help you see with new eyes what is so familiar to you, and hear with new ears what you've heard over and over at Mass so that you might respond well and be changed.

WHY THIS BOOK?

There are a number of books written with the goal of improving our understanding of the *ritual* of the Mass, by explaining its biblical roots, history or symbolism. Other books present theological insights or reflect on the correct way of celebrating Mass. Altogether, these books provide an invaluable service by deepening our appreciation for the mystery and majesty of the Mass.

But I have yet to find a book that examines the Mass, from beginning to end, as an *event*. That is what I do in this book. At Mass you are involved in a *ritual* that is an *event*. By looking at the Mass as an event, I focus on how it is a point of contact, communication and communion with Jesus Christ. I will show that Jesus Christ approaches you through the ritual in ways that will change your life. This approach does not negate the value of the Mass as a ritual. Rather, it shows how the ritual of the Mass is itself a *crucial event*.

THE GREATEST SHOW ON EARTH

At Mass, when we participate in the ritual Jesus Christ instituted at the Last Supper, we come into contact with an event greater than the "greatest show on earth." To be sure, the Mass is not a show, but during Mass, the greatest "showing up" on earth occurs. Why? Because Jesus Christ shows up at Mass in ways He does nowhere else. But He doesn't just show up. By His presence in the community, the Word, the priest and the Eucharist, He invites us to encounter *events* that are overwhelming in their majesty and power.

At Mass:

1. Jesus Christ includes you in His thanks and praise of God the Father, uniting Heaven and earth in one *Community* of thanksgiving and worship.

2. He communicates with you as *Word*, speaking the personal message you most need to hear at that moment.

3. He involves you in the crucial event where He is both *Priest* and Victim, called the Paschal Mystery (Jesus' Passion, death, Resurrection and Ascension).

4. He approaches you as Bread from Heaven, to be consumed by you in the *Eucharist* in order to transform you into Himself.

This is what happens at every Mass. In this book, I focus on these four encounters with Jesus Christ being offered to you. Your entire life is going to be changed. If only your eyes are open to see what is really happening. If only you have the ears to hear. If only you'll stop being a *spectator*. It's time to get off the sidelines and into the game. It's time to be a *participant*.

You tell me. Is this boring?

CHAPTER ONE

I ONCE WAS BLIND, BUT NOW I SEE

O my soul, created to enjoy such
exquisite gifts,
What are you doing, where is your
life going?
How wretched is the blindness of
Adam's children,
If indeed we are blind to such a
brilliant light
And deaf to so insistent a voice.

St. John of the Cross

A BLIND MAN ON HOLY GROUND

Late one morning a few years ago, I drove to a Catholic church near my office to pray. As I pulled into the parking lot, I noticed a hearse parked in front of the church and guessed that a funeral would begin soon. I decided to go in the side entrance and pray in an out-of-the-way alcove in the front of the church until the funeral started.

The alcove had only three or four rows of pews, and I knelt down to pray in the back row. Little did I know that the alcove was used for the final viewing of the deceased prior to a funeral. Shortly after I started praying, I looked up to see two ushers wheeling a closed casket into the alcove. They placed it in front of the first pew and left. Let's just say it was more than a bit distracting. Even so, it could have been worse; the casket could have been open.

You can guess what happened next. The two ushers came back into the alcove, opened the casket and prepared it for a final viewing. Not only that, but they set up a long, folding partition that blocked my view of the tabernacle and sanctuary. Then they left, leaving me alone with the mortal remains of a man at least 80 years old. I wondered whether the Lord had led me here to pray for this man. So I began praying for the repose of his soul. Two events happened in the minutes that followed; both involved people entering the alcove and viewing the body.

While I prayed quietly, two people entered the alcove: the funeral director and the woman whose husband was lying in the open casket. Upon seeing her husband, she began to gently fuss, "Oh, no, no, no." She adjusted his tie and pushed his hair off his forehead to one side like she had probably done so many times before. I was touched by the deep affection of this woman for her husband and her tender care for the details of his appearance, even in death.

Then the funeral director said solemnly, "I'll leave you alone" and left. The grieving widow was now alone with her husband ... and me. There I was, in an extraordinary position, watching a wife of 60 years looking on her husband for the last time on earth. I was on holy ground. What I was privileged to see was incredibly touching and heartbreaking all at once. I felt unworthy to be there as she gazed lovingly and painfully at her husband.

At that moment, she noticed she wasn't alone, that I was with her, kneeling in the last pew. When she looked at me, I said "Would you like me to leave?"

"No, no. It's fine." Then she turned back and looked again at her husband, and her composure gave way. She started to cry and very gently reached out and put her hand on his. This was no ordinary event; everything within me knew to act with utmost reverence. I was privileged to be at this holy moment and I was very careful not to desecrate it by anything I said or did. I wanted to watch, but at the same time felt compelled to avert my eyes. And that's exactly what I did. I put my head in my hands and prayed. I remained in that position until I heard her walk off. I will never forget my encounter with that event as long as I live.

That holy event would contrast greatly with what happened next. Knowing the widow had left the alcove,

I looked up to find myself alone once again with her deceased husband. Then I heard an interaction outside, with voices that were too loud to be appropriate in church. The source of the loud talking, an elderly couple, entered the alcove. I could tell immediately the man had trouble seeing and hearing. The man said in a loud voice, "Who was that?" (referring, of course, to the widow with whom they had just been talking). His wife replied in an equally loud voice, "That was Phyllis!" He responded abruptly and loudly, "Why didn't you tell me!" The wife retorted, "Keep your voice down! Everyone can hear you."

Ignoring his wife's last comment, he approached the open casket. He bent over it, straining to get as close as he could to try to see his deceased friend and said, "How does he look?" His wife replied, "He looks terrible." Unfortunately, she didn't speak loudly enough for him to hear, so he raised his voice, "What did you say?" She repeated herself in a louder voice, "Terrible. He looks terrible." To say the least, that was exactly how I was feeling as I witnessed what was happening in front of me.

Finally, the wife noticed me watching the two of them from the back pew. She quickly turned back to her husband, "Stop being so loud. There is a guy behind you hearing everything you're saying!" He turned around and stared at me through squinted eyes, "Who is he?" His wife replied, "I don't know." Immediately, I thought, *this* is an event I wished I never encountered. I got up and quickly left the church, feeling bad for that poor man. There he was, right in front of his deceased friend, but not seeing him. He was listening, but he could barely hear. The result? He missed a holy event.

Later, when I thought about the stunning contrast between these two encounters with the deceased man, a light came on. I saw a new connection between a saying of Jesus and the experience of being at Mass. Jesus spoke about those who have eyes but do not see and ears but do not hear (Matthew 13:13). What does this saying have to do with Mass? When I am at Mass, am I like the grieving widow who gazes lovingly upon her beloved, or the elderly man who could barely see or hear and missed the moment? Is Mass an event, a holy encounter with Jesus Christ who (unlike the man in the casket) is no longer dead but lives? Or do I look but not see, and listen but not hear the One present in the community, the Word, the priest and the Eucharist? At Mass do I encounter a dead ritual or a living Lord?

A dead ritual is boring. A living Lord is glorious. The Catholic Church teaches that Jesus Christ is present at every Mass in four ways. If so, then it's never a dead ritual, but an event, a place of vital contact with my living Lord. *If* I make contact! Maybe it's not that Mass is boring. Maybe the problem is on my side; that I miss the encounter with Jesus Christ because I don't see Him or hear His voice.

In the Gospel of John, chapter 9, Jesus cures a man "blind from birth" who then shares his good news with the Pharisees. They refuse to accept his explanation that Jesus healed his blindness. The chapter ends in the following way:

> Then Jesus said, "I came into this world for judgment, so that those who do not see might see, and those who do see might become blind." Some of the Pharisees who were with him heard this and said to him, "Surely we are not also blind, are we?" Jesus said to them, "If you were blind, you would have no sin; but now you are saying, 'We see,' so your sin remains." (John 9:39–41)

Seeing and hearing the Lord at Mass requires a supernatural intervention of God in our lives. This won't happen until we recognize we are also "blind from birth." Without God's grace we are incapable of encountering the Lord. We will be blind and deaf to Jesus Christ until He heals our eyes and ears.

Today, I am grateful to the Lord whenever I "see and hear" Him at Mass. Of course, having these encounters also points out how often I still miss the moment. I gratefully sing, "I once was blind, but now I see," and one thing I see better is how blind and deaf I continue to be at Mass. My need for God's healing, converting grace is ongoing.

There is a principle in Catholic theology that provides more insight here. "The quality of your recognition [i.e. your seeing and hearing] is made manifest by your response." First, notice that the principle draws attention to *how well* we see and hear, when it begins, "the *quality* of your recognition ..." In other words, like eyesight and hearing, for most people it's not a matter of either seeing or being blind, or hearing or being deaf. Our eyesight and hearing can improve or worsen. Similarly, our capacity to encounter (see and hear) Jesus Christ at Mass can and will increase or diminish.

Second, the principle teaches us a way to *measure* how well we see and hear "... is made manifest by your response." We respond by how we are *present* at Mass, how we *react* to the different parts of the Mass, and how *engaged* we are moment by moment. Our response shows us how well we truly see what's happening and who is there to meet us. Let me explain this principle more fully through a story.

SEEING MEANS RESPONDING

When my oldest daughter Mary Grace was just a few months old, I was sitting with my wife Kari on our couch on a Sunday afternoon watching a football game. Kari was holding Mary Grace, who was sick. At one point, Mary Grace became nauseous and Kari's shirt got the brunt of it.

Kari was a mess ... (Did I mention I was watching a football game?) She got up holding a dripping and crying Mary Grace at arms length and took her to the kitchen. She cleaned Mary Grace off at the sink, cleaned herself up, and then calmly carried Mary Grace back to the couch and sat down next to me again. "Tom, did you see what just happened?" I turned my head toward her, but my attention was still on the football game. It took a few moments to process her question. I was a bit puzzled. *Did I see what just happened?* Was this a trick question? Tentatively, I answered, "Yes, I saw what happened."

"Then why didn't you do anything to help me?"

A moment's reflection made me realize that there was no good answer to that question.

Did I see what just happened? Did I really recognize what occured while I was sitting right next to Kari and Mary Grace when she became nauseous?

To be sure, I *saw* what happened. I had eyes, but did I really see? The correct answer is that I did not see. My focus on the football game blinded me to what I should have focused on at that moment. I didn't "see" in the sense of *recognizing* what was really at stake in the *event* happening right before my eyes, when my sick daughter became nauseous and my wife needed help. If I had truly *recognized* what was happening, I would have *responded* differently. When Mary Grace got sick I should have jumped up immediately and said, "Kari, what can I do to help?" (And of course, turned off the TV!) What I *should* have done I didn't do. I failed to respond to the call of the moment. I failed to love as I ought. I wasn't "obedient" to what was being asked of me in that moment.

Obedience is an interesting word. The root meaning of the word in Latin is "to listen to." That shows the deep connection between *recognizing* and *responding*. Think about it, especially you parents of young children. How do you know that your children are *listening* to you? Of course, by whether or not they *obey* you. In fact, what do you say when your children don't obey? "You're not listening!" At those times, your kids have ears, they just aren't hearing. The quality of their recognition is manifested by their response.

What about at Mass? When my response to what I see and hear at Mass is "I'm bored," the problem lies with me. I am not recognizing what is really happening. I may know all the gestures and words by heart, I may follow along and respond correctly but I *miss the meaning*. I may be present at the ritual but miss the encounter.

Encountering Jesus Christ may elicit many "responses" from you; you may cry out in joy like the Apostle John upon recognizing the Risen Lord by the seashore, "It is the Lord!" (John 20:28). You may be knocked off your horse like the Apostle Paul, who was blinded by the light of God's glory (Acts 9:3–4). You may fall at His feet "as though dead" like the Apostle John in the Book of

Revelation (Revelation 1:17). There are many ways people have responded to encounters with the Risen Lord Jesus; being bored is not one of them. This brings up important questions. How does it happen that so many Catholics are bored at Mass? Why do so many Catholics have such poor eyesight and bad hearing when it comes to the Mass? Why do we respond so inadequately?

WHY DO WE SEE AND HEAR SO POORLY?

There are many answers to these questions, but I will share three reasons why I didn't see well or hear clearly at Mass:

1. I was at Mass because of someone else. I was physically present but I wasn't there because of my own personal decision to be present. I was there because of someone else's decision that I needed to be present.

2. For a time in my life, I lived as a "Cultural Catholic." That means I went to Mass because I was brought up Catholic, and going to Mass on Sunday is just what Catholics do. I went week after week without ever making any real effort to understand what was happening.

3. I did not want to commit a mortal sin. I went to Mass to "fulfill the obligation" to attend on Sunday. But my motivation went no deeper. (I'll admit I imagined the pit of hell as very deep, and avoiding it was a great motivator on some Sunday mornings.)

I know I am not alone in what I've just written. Many Catholics attend Mass because of one or more of these three reasons. I will explore what happens when we settle for reasons like these and then propose a deeper reason for attending Mass, one that will prepare us to encounter Jesus Christ.

RIGHT HERE, BUT A MILLION MILES AWAY

The first reason I listed above is that I went to Mass only because of someone else. This happens a lot with families who have school-age children. These are Catholics who, when asked whether and why they go to Mass will respond, "Of course I go to Mass. I take my whole family. It's important for the kids. That's why I go, for their sake." Ironically, if you talk with the kids in these families and ask them why they go to Mass, you will often hear, "I have no choice. My parents make me go. I'm only here because they force me to come to Mass with them." These families are *physically* present at Mass, but no one is making a personal decision to attend Mass because it's important to be there. None of them is there "for God's sake," for the sake of worshipping God, thanking God, honoring God and His Day. Nobody is *personally* present at Mass, though all are *physically* present. Is it surprising that both parents and kids will end up bored at Mass?

GOING THROUGH THE "CATHOLIC" MOTIONS

The second reason why I didn't see and hear what was really happening at Mass was because I was a "Cultural Catholic." My primary motivation for attending Mass on Sunday was "I am Catholic and that is what Catholics do on Sunday." Many Cultural Catholics attend Mass for years, even decades but most will gradually give up the regular practice of going to Mass. Why? A Cultural Catholic lives an unexamined life of faith. To paraphrase Socrates, the unexamined life of faith will not be worth living. I am not surprised that "Cultural Catholics" often end up as "former Catholics" or "inactive Catholics," a group that numbers in the tens of millions! When Mass doesn't connect to our lives, we will disconnect from the Mass and move on to find something else that does connect.

Let me illustrate what I mean. Can you imagine a guy who faithfully goes to football games, Sunday after Sunday, but has no clue about what is actually happening on the field? Imagine that the guy knows exactly how to act during the game. For example, when a player from the home team carries the ball across the thick white line at the end of the field, he knows it's time to stand up, clap and cheer loudly. He doesn't know *why* he is saying and doing that, but he recognizes that this is what he is supposed to do and he does it. Similarly, he knows that when a receiver on the home team is interfered with while trying to catch the football, he is to stand up and boo and yell at the referee if no yellow flag is thrown in the air. Our imaginary guy knows the right moment to yell "Blitz!" or "Screen!" He looks and acts like all the fans around him, but there are two crucial differences. The other fans *understand* the game of football and the *significance* of the actions on the field, and so they understand *why* they act and react the way they do to what's happening on the field.

I know this example is ridiculous. No one ignorant of what was happening on the football field would keep going to games, and just copy what other fans did. In real life, our guy would stop going to games ... or he would learn what was happening on the field so his reactions would not only be correct, but also meaningful. His passion and enthusiasm would be authentic and not mimicked.

The ignorant football fan is a figment of my imagination. Sadly, such is not the case with some (many? most?) who come to Mass. If the Mass is boring, it might be because we know the ritual from beginning to end, but don't understand the Mass or its meaning for our lives. We know when to stand up; we know when to sit down; we know the words to say; we know when to say them. We know what's expected of us outwardly and visibly, but we're missing the significance of the words and gestures. So even when we're responding in the way that we should (outwardly, visibly) we're not responding in the way that we should (from the heart, authentically, because we truly see). The result is that we miss the life-changing encounters with Jesus Christ and we're left with boredom.

MERE RULES OVER RELATIONSHIP

The third reason why I didn't see and hear what was really happening at Mass was because I was going to Mass only because I "had to." There are a large number of Catholics who go to Mass primarily because of the obligation to attend Mass on Sunday. It's one of the Ten Commandments. (Thou shalt keep holy the Lord's Day!) The difficulty is that when we settle for following the rule without understanding why the rule was made or what it really means, we are not likely to experience the Law as anything but a burden.

If you grew up Catholic like I did you probably learned "Catholic behaviors" or "Catholic rules" but maybe never were taught why they are there or what they mean. I knew the rules, but wasn't as clear about the relationship that was the *reason* for the rules. Eventually the rules felt a lot like an external burden. Pope Benedict XVI, prior to becoming pope, makes this point in striking language:

> Today, Christianity is seen as an old tradition, weighed down by old Commandments, something we already know which tells us nothing new; a strong institution, one of the great institutions that weigh on our shoulders. If we stay

with this impression, we do not live the essence of Christianity, which is an ever new encounter, an event thanks to which we can encounter the God who speaks to us, who approaches us, who befriends us. It is critical to come to this fundamental point of a personal encounter with God, who also today makes himself present, and who is contemporary. If one finds this essential center, one also understands all the other things. But if this encounter is not realized, which touches the heart, all the rest remains like a weight, almost like something absurd.[1]

Our Holy Father makes clear that the Commandments are all about our relationship with God; about having a personal encounter with the Father through the Son in the Spirit. Going to Mass on Sunday only to fulfill the Commandment misses the point of the Commandment and the Mass, which is the relationship. The Commandments offer us guardrails to keep us on the right path, not prison bars that make us feel trapped.

We've explored three reasons for going to Mass that fail to prepare us for life-giving encounters with Jesus Christ. What reason for going to Mass will stir us and

---

1. *Cardinal Ratzinger Tells Why Many Misperceive Christianity,* May 6, 2004, http://www.zenit.org/ article-10033?l=english

awaken us to the presence and action of Jesus Christ at Mass? I can give you the answer in one word: Eucharist.

ENTER HIS GATES WITH THANKSGIVING

Sometimes Mass is called a Celebration of the Holy Eucharist. Do you know what the word "Eucharist" means? Growing up Catholic, when I heard the word Eucharist I thought of the Host consecrated by the priest at Mass. What I didn't know was that Eucharist comes from a Greek word that means "Thanksgiving."

Thanksgiving; have you ever thought about that? It is the first answer to the question, "Why am I going to Mass?" I go to Mass in order to give thanks to God. The second answer is to praise. Those are the fundamental reasons why I should be at Mass, to thank and praise God. In the next chapter, I will focus on how we praise and worship God at Mass. Here, I offer a brief reflection on the irreplaceable way that Mass gives us a chance to thank God.

I AM FOREVER IN YOUR DEBT

I once read that the day of the year when the most phone calls are made is Mother's Day. It makes sense. A phone call is a small way we acknowledge that our parents have given us something more precious and greater in magnitude than anything we could ever give them in return. They gave us life. No matter what else we received from them, good or bad, simply because we are alive, we owe our parents a debt of gratitude.

What about God; do you acknowledge what He has given you? How regularly do you express your gratitude to God? How concerned are you to adequately and appropriately give God thanks? I ask myself these questions often, because I often take for granted all of the incredible blessings God has given me and those I love. I am challenged by the Psalmists. For them, giving thanks to God is a burning concern in the core of their being. "How can I make a return to the Lord for all the good He has done for me?" (Psalm 116:12). I wonder if I have given "thanks to the Lord with all my heart" the way the Psalmists do. What about you?

Have you ever felt a pain in your heart because of your inability to adequately express your gratitude to God? Have you ever felt an urgent longing to find a way, some way, any way to thank God in the manner that He deserves? If so, you are not alone. How enormous is the debt of gratitude we owe to God? Let's consider the facts. Begin by thinking about all the good things God has given us. Here is the truth: God has given us all that we are and have. Even more than our parents, God has given us life.

What about all the good things in our lives that we are tempted to take for granted: food, a home, work, health, safety, medical care, family, people who love you, friends, your faith? Even if you don't have all of those good things, do you realize the precious gift you have received when you have faith in God? Not everyone has that gift! And not only faith, but when we disobey God, we are offered mercy. When we confess our sins we are forgiven, even though we don't deserve it. The list of all that we continuously and undeservedly receive from God is almost endless, and the debt, immeasurable.

THROUGH HIM, WITH HIM AND IN HIM

So, how can we thank God adequately, in a way He deserves? The short answer is: we can't. At least not by ourselves. We are finite creatures and God is infinite. On top of that, you and I are fallen creatures whose sins render our thanksgiving to God tainted and inauthentic. We all know this by experience, or at least we should. So how do we, fallen, imperfect, finite creatures, show our gratitude to God in a way that He deserves? How do we do the impossible? There is only one way. *Through*, *with* and *in* the One Who is The Way: Jesus Christ. He makes all things possible.

How? By linking your act of thanksgiving to His. Simply stated, when you speak words of thanksgiving at Mass, God the Father hears the voice of God the Son. At Mass, Jesus Christ is Himself offering the perfect prayer of thanks to His Father. The Mass is the place where you encounter Jesus Christ. He is not only present but active. At Mass, you enter *His* "Eucharistic act," His act of Thanksgiving. Mass is first of all an act of Jesus Christ, and because of Him, His Body the Church is also active. As a member of the Church, your voice is joined with His, so that you pray in your own voice but not on your own. You pray "through Him, with Him and in Him" that "all glory and honor are Yours, Almighty Father, forever and ever." Amen!

That's what happens at Mass. You finally get to pay your debt of gratitude to God. Have you ever wondered what was so special about going to Mass? Why can't you just stay home and thank God in your room or as you walk in the woods? Here's your answer: you go to Mass to pay your debt of gratitude to God. To thank God in a way that is fitting and in a way that He deserves. If you are not interested in that or find that boring, then I give up, and you will probably also give up going to Mass. But if you realize all that God continuously gives you freely, and you have any inclination at all to try to thank God in a way that He deserves, you have the reason you need to get out of bed, get ready and go to Mass.

CHAPTER TWO

JESUS CHRIST PRESENT IN THE COMMUNITY

When I consider how my light is spent
E're half my days, in this dark world and wide,
And that one Talent which is death to hide,
Lodg'd with me useless, though my Soul more bent
To serve therewith my Maker, and present
My true account, least he returning chide,
Doth God exact day-labour, light deny'd,
I fondly ask; But patience to prevent
That murmur, soon replies, God doth not need
Either man's work or his own gifts, who best
Bear his milde yoak, they serve him best, his State
Is Kingly. Thousands at his bidding speed
And post o're Land and Ocean without rest:
They also serve who only stand and waite.

John Milton, On His Blindness

BEING ON YOUR TOES

When I am driving home at the end of a long day of work, the odds are pretty good that as I turn onto my street, I will see some of my kids looking out the upstairs window of our home. As they recognize my car, they jump up and down and wave excitedly, their mouths wide open in screams of excitement. Their wait is over. Dad is home! They race to the front door to meet me with hugs and kisses. I love it.

What if we went to Mass with my kids' attitude? Expectant waiting. Excitement at the thought of the imminent arrival of a loved one. If we went to Mass with that attitude, we'd be on the edge of our pews. That idea isn't as strange as it might first sound. At Mass, you are meant to encounter the Lord of the Universe, your loving God, Who is coming to speak to you, and if you have prepared yourself for the encounter, if you are open and receptive to Christ's approach, if you have the eyes to see and ears to hear, your life will be changed.

If you are like me, when you realize there's a lot at stake at a particular moment, you pay special attention. Like when I played baseball in my youth. When I played third base and the next batter was likely to bunt, I was on my toes, looking for the merest sign that the batter was going to square himself to the pitcher in order to bunt. I was focused, ready. I couldn't afford to let my attention wander. Everything hinged on my being alert and responding immediately when the batter made his move.

What about Mass? When I get bored at Mass or my attention wanders, I've forgotten what is at stake in that moment, and so I am not "on my toes" with expectant waiting. What's at stake at Mass is missing out on the approach of Jesus Christ or failing to respond in accord with what He asks from us. When we learn how to "be on the lookout" for Jesus Christ at Mass; when the Mass is no longer just a ritual that repeats the same old thing every time, but becomes an event through which we encounter Jesus Christ, then it will be anything but boring.

TIME FOR AN ATTITUDE ADJUSTMENT

When I am bored at Mass, I know exactly what I need: an attitude adjustment. I need to recover an attitude of expectant waiting for the encounter with Jesus Christ. The theological word for this is conversion. I need a radical change of mind set, a new attitude. I need to let go of attitudes that leave me blind and deaf, and welcome the attitude that makes me attentive and ready to meet Jesus Christ. What I have found is that when I get bored, it is most often because I have taken on an attitude of an *uninterested spectator* or a *critical observer* at Mass and given up an attitude of *alert readiness*. What do I mean by these attitudes or ways of being present at Mass?

I will explain by giving you an example from my relationship with Kari. There are a few times in my married life when Kari has approached me and said, "We need to talk. There is something really important I want to share with you." When I hear these words, I realize something's going on inside Kari. And here is the key to all that follows. Whether or not I discover what's in her heart will depend mostly on my attitude, on how I choose to be present to Kari. I can choose an attitude of an *uninterested spectator,* a *critical observer,* or an attitude of *alert readiness.*

I am smart enough to know that it is never the right answer to treat Kari's request like an uninterested spectator, so I'll just move on to the second attitude, being a critical observer. That was the attitude I chose the first couple of times Kari approached me with a desire to share deeply with me. I would hear her request and then stand back and try to analyze things objectively. I would dissect and critique the situation to try and figure out what she wanted to say to me. I would ask myself questions like: What did Kari say or not say, do or not do, recently? What about me? What did I do or say recently? What about the calendar; what day is it? How does Kari look right now? What can I tell from looking at Kari's face, her demeanor, her mood and her tone of voice? I would then try to piece together all these bits of data and formulate a conclusion about what Kari wanted to say. If you've been married for more than a few years, I'll bet you're smiling at this. How likely were my attempts to analyze Kari going to correctly identify what Kari wanted to talk to me about? Not likely at all. It never worked even once. I never discovered what was hidden in Kari's heart by remaining at a distance from her and critically observing and analyzing the situation. And I thought I was pretty good at it!

When I engage in critical analysis, I am choosing to stand apart from a situation. I dissect what I see by breaking it down into pieces, and then arrive at conclusions. Critical analysis by its very nature makes me into an observer, a *spectator*, often a critic, but never a participant. Think about it; you can only dissect what is dead. The heart of a woman must be approached differently. It took me a few years, but I finally realized having the attitude of a *critical observer* was never going to work.

CRITICS MISS THE ENCOUNTER

When Kari said she had something to talk to me about that was very important, I had a third possibility. I could choose an attitude of *alert readiness*. I could be present to Kari with an open, attentive stance. It is a way of being present that says, "I love you. I am here with you. I am open to what you have to say. I want to hear what you want to share. Please, open your heart and reveal what is hidden there." (Newly married men, you might want to write some of this down or underline it for future reference.)

But I had to do more than just say those words. I had to display that attitude in how I was present to her. That meant shutting off the TV, (you can't have conversations like this during commercials or half-time; trust me) and focusing only on Kari. My attitude towards Kari shows up in my demeanor and mood, by the look in my eye and the way I sit in front of her. All of these things are part of expressing an attitude of alert readiness. But note something very important. This attitude isn't just about being alert and ready; it's about love. I choose this attitude because of what Kari means to me, who she is in my life. Because I love Kari, I want her to know that I am open and ready to listen attentively. What is astonishing is what happens next. In seeing my openness to her, Kari will not only choose to share what is important and hidden in her heart, but in her act of sharing what's in her heart, she will be invited by my attitude to share her very self with me. That's what love is; self-donation. As Pope John Paul II taught so beautifully, to love is to give yourself as a gift. If I remain an aloof analyst or critical observer, I can try to figure out all day what Kari wants to tell me, and I may even get some of it right. But I will miss what is most important of all; I will miss her sharing of herself with me. If I am not open to her, I will entirely miss the encounter with Kari. The critical observer misses personal encounters. The alert, receptive person is ready for them.

AVOIDING THE CRITICAL MASS

Can you see how this explanation of these three attitudes applies to our experience of Mass? It makes all the difference in the world if I come to Mass as an uninterested spectator, critical observer or with alert readiness. The wrong attitude will close me off from meeting Jesus Christ. Almost without exception, I do an attitude check as I'm entering the church. What attitude do I have right now? If I hope to have life-changing, personal encounters with Jesus Christ at Mass, I need to have an attitude of *alert readiness;* and above all, this needs to be rooted in my love for Jesus Christ. Too often I settle for less. When I allow myself to fall into the attitude of a *critical observer* or worse, an *uninterested spectator,* I will not experience the personal encounter Jesus intended for me at that Mass.

Think about your own attitude. Whether you are sitting or standing at Mass, what is your typical thought process? If you are like me, your inclination (or well-established habit) is to analyze what is happening, making critical observations about a myriad of easy targets around the church. Do you ever find yourself evaluating how that lady is dressed, how that family is acting, what the priest said or left out, how the lector pronounced that word in the First Reading, what the banners look like, the choice of music or how it was sung? It goes on and on. There are so many temptations to drag us away from an attitude of alert readiness back into the attitude of the critical observer. If we settle for the attitude of the analyst, the critical observer, it's no wonder we've had few life-changing, personal encounters with Jesus Christ at Mass. It's understandable that Mass would have little impact on our lives. But we don't have to settle for this. We can strive for a new attitude. We can work on being more alert and attentive. We bring our love for God to bear on how we approach Mass. We can prepare ourselves for a different way of relating to what happens at Mass. That's the goal of the rest of this book.

I am going to walk through the Mass with you, and try to be *alert* and *ready* to recognize and respond to what (and Who) is showing up. I'm not going to spend a lot of ink analyzing the Mass by critically examining things like the color of the priest's vestment, or why we have candles, or things like that. That would be essential if my goal were to provide you with more information about the Mass. But gaining more and more information might only make you an even more *critical* observer. Ironically, becoming more of an expert on the meaning of the Mass can have the effect of making us even harsher critics, rather than increasing in us an alert readiness to meet Jesus Christ that is rooted in love. My goal is to help you gain insight rather than information, to gain new "sight into" the Mass. Taking up the attitude of alert readiness I've been discussing in this chapter will help you accomplish this. We will be on the lookout for encounters with Jesus Christ available to us at every Mass. Our goal is to not only *recognize* these encounters, but to understand how to *respond* to them. If you respond well, your life will be changed.

WHERE ON EARTH DO I GET A GLIMPSE OF HEAVEN?

As you enter the church on Sunday, chances are you are not thinking, "I'm about to have four encounters with Jesus that just might change my life!" But being made aware that Jesus is waiting to meet you, you will most certainly ask, "Where is He?" Look around you. Jesus Christ is present in the community gathered at Mass. Yes, that's right. Those other folks hurrying and making their way to their "assigned" pews. Jesus Christ intends to encounter you at Mass in them. But not only in them. If we pay attention to the clues the Church gives us we discover that the community present at Mass is, in fact, much bigger than the people who happen to be in the church building filling the pews, the priest, lectors, Eucharistic ministers and servers. What are some of those clues?

The first clue is found in our own hearts before we even enter the church. How many of us feel God really knows us personally and cares for the details of our lives? The right answer is, not enough! We want to know that God is real and that He cares, but God is in Heaven, and Heaven seems vague and distant. But is it? What if you knew a place where an event happened that brought Heaven to earth, caused earth to be drawn into Heaven, and brought you into God's very presence? What would you want to do? I don't know about you, but I would want to make sure that I was ready for the occasion.

BLESSING YOURSELF

What do we do before we even enter the church? We automatically look for the holy water font to bless ourselves. We have done this so often, so naturally and quickly that we may not have thought about the meaning of this gesture. So, let me ask you, why do you bless yourself? Stop and think about it. You don't bless yourself at a holy water font before entering a bowling alley, or to eat at McDonalds, or to go to work. You don't see holy water fonts at the entrances of malls (but maybe we should!) But here, in *this* place, before entering the church building to participate in Mass, we bless ourselves with holy water. We make the sign of the cross as a way of recognizing we are about to enter holy ground, not just a religious building. We are preparing to participate in a holy event. Get ready, be alert. We are entering into the presence of God.

Entering a Catholic church when Mass is about to begin is no ordinary space. At Mass we are entering into that place on earth where Heaven breaks in. Here at Mass, earth will be drawn into Heaven, and time into eternity. The everlasting worship of angels and saints around the throne of God is breaking into time and space. This is what happens at every Mass. Remember the principle I introduced earlier? The quality of your recognition is made manifest by your response. If we casually or mindlessly wander into Mass, what does that say about our recognition of what event is about to take place, where that event will bring us and who is going to be there with us? It says we need to get our eyesight checked.

The Church is trying to help improve your vision about what happens at Mass by placing the holy water font in front of you. By blessing yourself with holy water, and making the sign of the cross you are asking the Lord to grace you with a cleansed mind and heart as you prepare to meet Him in Mass. But you also bless yourself as a reminder of your Baptism when you were "plunged and immersed" (that's what the word "baptism" actually means) into the Passion, death and Resurrection of Jesus. You recall the event whereby you were cleansed from all your sins and welcomed into the Body of Christ as an adopted son or daughter of God. All of that is expressed in the simple act of blessing yourself with holy water.

DRAWN UP TO HEAVEN

Now that we've blessed ourselves, let's walk into the church and look around. What do you see?

Many older churches are structured so that when we walk in we notice the expansiveness, the openness, and the height of the ceiling. This makes no sense from an economic perspective. Look at any church's heating bill and you will see that it is not a very efficient design. Why all that vast expanse of vaulted ceiling? The church is structured like this so that when you walk in your head and heart will be drawn upwards toward Heaven. In fact, in many older churches, all of the activity, all of the angels, all of the pictures, all of the stained glass windows are high up on the wall or on the ceiling. What is down below is plain or unadorned.

We are being led by the very architecture of the building to realize that while we are at Mass, the reality of Heaven is breaking in. The artwork also points us to Heaven. The statues, frescoes and paintings of angels and saints are meant not only to inspire us, but to remind us who is present with us. At Mass, we are drawn into the "community" of those who worship God in Heaven— angels, archangels, saints, virgins, martyrs, the honorable company of the prophets, the glorious company of the apostles and the Mother of God—the "great cloud of witnesses" that Scripture speaks of:

> No, you have approached Mount Zion and the city of the living God, the heavenly Jerusalem, and countless angels in festal gathering, and the assembly of the firstborn enrolled in heaven, and God the judge of all, and the spirits of the just made perfect, and Jesus, the mediator of a new

covenant, and the sprinkled blood that speaks more eloquently than that of Abel.

(Hebrews 12:22–24)

The next time you enter a Catholic church to go to Mass, think of the immense throng you are joining, giving thanks and praise to God at every Mass.

HEAVEN SHINES THROUGH

Many churches have stained glass windows. How does a stained glass window work? From the outside, it is not very impressive. Ordinarily, it is dark, the images obscure. Stained glass windows only work from the inside. Not only that, they only work during the day when the sun is out. It is only when there is light on the outside streaming in that stained glass windows have the intended effect. When they are lit up, incredible images of saints, biblical scenes, or God Himself, are displayed, stirring our minds and hearts. But if you are in the church at night or when there is little light outside, the most beautiful, astonishing stain glass windows will appear dull, flat and meaningless. They will certainly not capture your attention. There is a lesson here for us about the Mass. Mass only works when we recognize the light of Heaven shining through the ritual. If we are blind to this light, the Mass will appear dull, flat and meaningless. It will certainly not capture our attention. If we are open to the light, with the sight that faith brings, we will come to stand in awe at the light of Heaven that radiates and shines forth as Mass unfolds.

TAKE A KNEE

At Mass we are welcomed into the presence of God. The holy water font prepares us, and the art, architecture and stained glass windows deepen our awareness of God's presence. Then, we do something else that points to the fact that Jesus Christ is present in the church in an extraordinary way. Before entering the pew, we make an unusual gesture: we genuflect, lowering our right knee to the floor, pausing and then standing up. Growing up, I couldn't even imagine going into a pew without genuflecting. Today, it's hit or miss. Why? Some contemporary church buildings are constructed with a separate space for the tabernacle outside the main body of the church. In those churches, people don't genuflect when entering a pew, only when entering the place where the Blessed Sacrament is reserved.

Have you ever thought about how unusual it is to perform this action? Where else in your week do you make that gesture? Probably nowhere. (Unless you're picking up after your kids!) I was taught from my earliest years that I genuflected before entering the pew as a way of acknowledging the presence of Jesus Christ in the Blessed Sacrament reserved in the tabernacle. But why is going down on one knee an appropriate way to acknowledge

His presence in the tabernacle? Why not wave? Do you go down on one knee when you come into the presence of friend, loved one or boss? Why is it significant that we genuflect? Old movies help us here.

Remember those classic movies about the Roman Empire? There is almost always a scene where a soldier in the Roman legion strides confidently into the presence of the Caesar, or some important commanding officer, and right before addressing him he drops to a knee and bows his head. He genuflects! By this gesture, the soldier acknowledges he has come into the presence of his lord, the one whose word is obeyed without question or hesitation. He is expressing his complete subjection to the authority of his commander.

Genuflecting before entering the pew has the potential to be a powerful way of expressing who Jesus Christ is in your life. When we genuflect, we can be saying something significant, "Jesus, I acknowledge that I have come into Your presence, You who are my Lord, my Commander. I submit myself completely to Your authority. I express before the entire community, and especially to You right now, that whatever You command, I will do. I am Yours."

We are acknowledging Jesus' presence in the midst of our community. Remember the principle: the quality of our recognition is made manifest by our response. So many Catholics faithfully perform gestures during Mass without recognizing their meaning. Genuflection is a habit ingrained in us from our youth, but not as a sign of submission to the authority of our Lord who is present. I encourage you to come up with a short, simple prayer like the one above that you can speak to yourself every time you genuflect. It will help an old habit take on fresh meaning. It will become what it was intended to be: an authentic expression of your recognition that you have entered into the presence of Jesus Christ, the Lord of the Universe, the Master of History, the Redeemer of the world and your Savior.

OUR MISERY AND GOD'S MAJESTY

Having been educated by the holy water font, church art and architecture, the gestures of blessing ourselves and genuflecting, and hopefully with a few minutes of silent prayer and getting settled, we are ready to begin Mass. We stand as the priest processes in. He leads us in making the sign of the cross, "In the Name of the Father, and of the Son and of the Holy Spirit," and then addresses us with an expression we will hear several times at Mass, "The Lord be with you." These first two statements of the priest point out that we are not gathering alone; we are in the presence of God as we perform this ritual. The Lord *is* with us. Because we are involved in a ritual that brings us into God's presence in a special way, the priest asks us to do something that acknowledges God's presence. What does he ask us to do? To think about our sins: "Let us call to mind our sins."

This does not seem like a very warm or inviting way to begin. How many of us have had friends over for dinner and said, "Hi, Frank, great to have you over. Before we go any further, take a moment and think about your sins and failings. Then confess them and ask for my prayers." You know what Frank would do in real life; he would be on his way out the door in two seconds flat. So why does the Church ask us to do this? The saints give us the answer. They teach us that when we are drawn into the presence of the all-holy God, what we become aware of immediately is that we are far from being all holy, that we have sinned. Mass begins with a clear indication that we are in fact in God's presence in a special way. When we stand in the bright spotlight of God's holiness, we become instantly aware of the darkness in our lives; we recognize our sins and failings quickly and unavoidably. The ritual of the Mass gives us words to say called the *Confiteor*, ("I confess" in Latin) that respond to that recognition:

> I confess to almighty God,
> and to you, my brothers and sisters,
> that I have sinned through my own fault,
> in my thoughts and in my words,
> in what I have done,
> and in what I have failed to do;
> and I ask blessed Mary, ever virgin,

all the angels and saints,

and you, my brothers and sisters,

to pray for me to the Lord our God.

From the very first words and actions of the Mass, we are saying things that indicate we are in God's presence in a way that isn't ordinary. We recognize that there is a special manner of God's presence at Mass that causes us to respond by praying the *Confiteor*. The *Confiteor* itself clarifies how special that presence of God is when we ask for prayers not only from those on earth with us in the pews, but also from those in Heaven, the angels and the saints. The special presence of God we experience at Mass is not a presence of God alone, but of God and His angels and saints.

I've been sharing with you insights that point out that Christ's presence in the community at Mass extends far beyond the community of those on earth and includes the angels and saints in Heaven. The prayer we just prayed confirms this insight in a very powerful way. Whom are you addressing when you pray this prayer? Of course, you are addressing God, but did you notice you also speak directly to the Blessed Virgin Mary, and all the angels and saints? How can you ask the Blessed Virgin Mary or all the angels and saints anything unless *they are with us?* We are actually asking not just the people here in the pew next to us to pray for us, but also and first of all the Blessed Virgin Mary, and all the angels and saints. We address those present in Heaven as if they are right there in church with us, and they are! Our Blessed Mother Mary sitting next to you, Saint Paul right there next to John, angels and saints, your loved ones that have gone before you marked with the sign of faith. They are all present with us at Mass.

GLORY TO GOD IN THE HIGHEST—
RIGHT HERE ON EARTH

We confess our sinfulness because we are drawn into the presence of infinite holiness. But more important than focusing on our misery, is acknowledging God's infinite majesty. That is why, after we confess our sinfulness, but intimately connected with it, we confess or proclaim God's glory. How do we start the *Gloria?* "Glory to God in the Highest, and peace to His people on earth." You probably recognize that line from the story of the shepherds and the angels at the birth of Jesus in the Gospel of Luke. At Mass, we not only are joined with those in Heaven, we pray in a heavenly manner. We are given the words of angels. We make them our own. We sing "Glory to God in the Highest," because we are lifted up to Heaven to participate in what the angels are unendingly doing: praising God's glory.

God's glory is majestic and beautiful beyond what words will ever be able to tell, even given all eternity to do it! What causes the angels and saints to cry out "Glory!" with maximum joy, wonder and awe is simultaneously being said on earth at Mass by so many of us in a lack-luster, inattentive, half-hearted way. Why? As I've already said, "the quality of our recognition is made manifest by our response." How we pray the *Confiteor* and the *Gloria* will show just how deep our recognition is that we have been granted access to Heaven at Mass, and that we are in the presence of angels and saints asking them for prayers and glorifying God with them. At Mass, God makes room for us around His heavenly throne. The more lively our awareness of this, the less likely that we will ever be bored at Mass again.

In this chapter I have tried to help you see that Christ's presence in the community at Mass introduces us to an encounter with God's presence that is so profound that Heaven breaks into earth, and earth is drawn into Heaven. We are invited into the very thanks and praise Jesus Christ, our great High Priest, offers to the Father. Having moved through the *Greeting, Penitential Rite,* and the *Gloria,* we now come to the *Collect,* where the priest, his arms opened in the stance of prayer, "collects" or gathers into one the aspirations and prayers of the community. After our agreement (Amen!) with his prayer, we move into the *Liturgy of the Word*, the part of the Mass where we will be invited to have our second life-giving encounter with Jesus Christ: His presence in the *proclaimed Word.*

CHAPTER THREE

JESUS CHRIST PRESENT IN THE WORD

The Word of God may well require
something of me today it had not
demanded yesterday; consequently, in
order to perceive this demand, I must,
in the depths of my being, be open and
attentive to the Word. No relationship
is closer ... than that between the
man in grace and the Lord who gives
grace, between the Head and the body,
between the vine and the branch. But this
relationship can only have full play if it
prevails, too, in the realm of the spirit,
that is if the freedom of the Word is
answered by a corresponding readiness
on the part of man to hear, to follow and
to comply.

Hans Urs von Balthasar

CAN I HAVE A WORD WITH YOU?

Having been drawn into the presence of God, we have confessed our sins and praised God's glory with the angels and saints in heaven. We do so because Jesus Christ is present in our midst gathering us together in a community that extends from earth to Heaven.

Now we begin the first of the two main parts of Mass, called the *Liturgy of the Word*. This part of the Mass includes the two *Readings, Responsorial Psalm, Gospel, Homily, Profession of Faith* and *Prayers of the Faithful*. We have just focused on the meaning of Jesus Christ's presence in the community. Now we shift our focus to the presence of Jesus Christ in the proclaimed "Word of the Lord." Here is the second opportunity we have to encounter Jesus Christ in a way that will change our lives. Let's pay attention to what happens during the *Liturgy of the Word* and see what we need to do to recognize and respond to Jesus Christ present in the Word.

THEY ALSO SERVE WHO ONLY SIT AND WAIT

As the *Liturgy of the Word* begins, we do something so commonplace that we probably don't consider it significant. What do we do? We sit down. Why is sitting down significant? To answer the question, recall first of all why we are at Mass: to give thanks and praise to God in union with the Son of God Himself. In fact, we have just begun to do this very thing by confessing our sins and God's glory. Standing feels right if our goal is to praise and worship God. Compared to standing, sitting down seems like "sitting out" or taking a break from the action. So why do we sit?

We sit because the direction of the Mass changes from emphasizing what we are doing (gathering, confessing, praising, thanking, singing), to emphasizing what God is doing (speaking). By sitting, rather than standing, we are appropriately responding to this moment in the Mass. It's as if God is saying to us, "Please sit down, I have something to say to you. You are here to praise and thank me, but right now, I want to come close to you and talk to you." So we stop praising and thanking Him and start listening to Him. Or better yet, we express our praise and thanks by honoring His request. We sit down and listen.

When comparing standing and sitting, it's natural to think of standing as an active and alert posture, and sitting as a passive or inactive posture. That may be true in other settings like watching television; sit too long and get ready to be called a couch potato. That sounds pretty passive to me. At Mass, sitting has a different meaning. Sitting is not an invitation to "sit back and relax" during the Readings; the opposite is expected from us. I am sad to admit how many times I've zoned out during the Readings because of my couch potato attitude and completely missed out on the personal encounter with Jesus Christ that awaited me at that moment. What should we do to stop zoning out during the Readings? We do the same as we did regarding recognizing the presence of the Lord in the community, we make an attitude adjustment.

COUCH POTATO OR CATCHER?

There is an alternative to being a couch potato; we can have the attitude of a baseball catcher. We can ready ourselves to receive, like a catcher poised and waiting for a fastball from a pitcher who's begun his windup. The catcher is the only player on the baseball diamond not standing, but he is the most alert and expectant player on the field. That's the attitude we can have as we listen to the two Readings and the Gospel. Sitting during the Readings can be a moment when we are poised and ready to receive a Word from the Lord. The Readings are a time to tune in rather than zone out.

What I've described is a way of sitting similar to the way Mary of Bethany sat at the feet of Jesus while her sister Martha was busy doing many things. Martha complained to Jesus because Mary was doing nothing but sitting. Jesus told Martha she was wrong. Mary was not "doing nothing"—she was active in a way that was different than Martha. She was actively hanging on every word that Jesus spoke. She was attentive and alert to "catch" what Jesus said, and Jesus praised her for it. In fact, He identified her as choosing "the one thing necessary" and "the better part." (Luke 10:38–42)

As the "Word of the Lord" is proclaimed, Jesus is inviting you to do the "one thing necessary" and receive "the better part" by sitting and listening with open ears like Mary. This is what disciples traditionally did; they *sat* at the feet of their Rabbi to listen to his teaching. Jesus Christ is asking, "Can I have a word with you?" During this part of the Mass, He wants you to encounter Him as *Word*, as One Who has a message just for you. In order to grab hold of His message, we need to have the attitude of the catcher, an attitude of readiness to receive, an alert and expectant listening on the edge of our seats. That's what sitting means.

KNOCK! KNOCK!

There is another reason why encountering Jesus Christ in the Readings is going to be difficult for us. It has to do with our experience of books. When we read books, we are active (we are doing the reading) and the words on the page are passive (the words are being read). But the Church, by having us sit, is asking us to recognize that the Bible is unlike any other book. The Bible is God's Word in human words; other books are just humans' words. Reading is our normal way of actively engaging with a book, but when that book is the Bible, we are active in a different way. We are actively listening, because the Word of the Lord is being spoken. As it says in Hebrews 4:12, the Word of God is "living" and "active."

As the father of seven children I can tell you about active books, because we have many. Open one of them up and an animal pops out at you. Pull a handle and music turns on, or the wheels on the bus go round and round. Lift this panel; scratch and sniff. Books like this are engaging; they interact with you. But when I say the Bible is active, I mean to say that it engages you and inter-acts with you in much more profound ways than any kid's book. Our interaction is not with the words printed on the page, but with a divine *Person, the Word Who is God,* Who encounters us through, with and in those words. For many Catholics, maybe for you, this is a new idea. If so, be patient, because it's going to take some time getting used to relating to the Bible differently than other books.

Why do I say that? Too few Catholics have developed a way of relating to the Bible as the "living" and "active" Word of God. If you were like me, you were first taught about the Bible as a *book to be studied.* Maybe you went to a Bible Study where you learned lots of information about a particular book of the Bible; about the author, the historical circumstances of the writing, the book's literary style, central message, key themes, etc. That's not bad. In fact it is essential. But it fosters in us a way of relating to the Bible that makes us active and the Bible passive. The Bible is treated as a dead letter rather than a living

Word. There is no encounter with Jesus Christ, the Word of God, if the only way you relate to the Bible is as a book to be studied.

Later on, I remember reading a different kind of Bible Study, one primarily interested in "life application." These studies presented the Bible as an *Owner's Manual* for living a godly life. Readers were asked to read a passage, discover the biblical principle and then think about ways to apply that principle to their lives. This is also very useful, especially in times like ours when truth is considered to be subjective. But again, if we relate to the Bible as a divinely inspired Owner's Manual, we will not expect or seek an encounter with Jesus Christ when we read it.

Though these are valuable ways to use the Bible, in our Catholic tradition, the first and most important way of relating to the Bible is as a *place of encounter*. We read the Bible to meet the Author, God Himself. That's interaction! We can do this because Jesus Christ is the Word of God Who is made manifest in human words. How do we relate to the Bible as a place of encounter? By using it in the context of prayer. Prayer always begins with God's initiative. As it says in Isaiah 45:4, *I have called you by your name.* By opening your Bible and praying in a spirit of faith, you are not initiating contact with God but responding to His personal call. Behold, He stands at the door and knocks! (Revelation 3:20). If you recognize His voice and "open up the door," expect that He will communicate with you in and through His Holy Word. This is especially true in liturgical prayer, like the Mass. The Word of God's natural home is the Mass, where the Word is proclaimed and we are in the posture of listeners, of those ready to encounter the Author.

It might be helpful to think of reading the Bible less like reading a book and more like answering a door when someone knocks, or answering a phone when someone calls. When someone knocks at your door and you open it, what do you expect? You expect someone to *be* there. When you get a phone call and you answer it, what do you expect? You expect to hear a voice. To *not* hear a voice when you answer your phone would be odd. To open your door and find nobody there would be strange. And yet, that is often our expectation when the reading of the Word of the Lord happens at Mass. What do you typically expect during the Readings? To meet the Lord and have Him communicate with you or not? What would surprise you more?

PIERCED BY A TWO-EDGED SWORD

At Sunday Mass, we sit for the First and Second Readings. They are proclaimed to us; we don't read them quietly to ourselves. We are seated not only in our pews, but at the Lord's feet. Jesus Christ is not just speaking to a crowd; He is speaking to you, and He has a word just for you. It is a personal word that speaks to you right where you are in your life situation. Earlier, I referenced Hebrews where it mentions the Word as living and active. Here are the verses in their entirety:

> Indeed the word of God is living and effective, sharper than any two-edged sword, penetrating even between soul and spirit, joints and marrow, and able to discern reflections and thoughts of the heart. No creature is concealed from him, but everything is naked and exposed to the eyes of him to whom we must render an account.
> (Hebrews 4:12–13)

God's Word proclaimed at Mass is a two-edged sword that has the power to sever the bonds of fear and anxiety that hold us captive, to pierce the darkness that clouds our minds, and to cut loose the burdens that weigh on our hearts. Even more, the Word can expose our sinful attitudes, heal our hidden wounds and bring us a peace that nothing in this world can match. One popular way of saying this is that at Mass the Word proclaimed will comfort the afflicted and afflict the comfortable.

ENCOUNTERING THE HEART OF CHRIST

At Mass we are invited to have a life-changing encounter with Jesus Christ, who is the Word proclaimed. And His Word is the Truth that will set us free. In Greek, the word for truth is *aletheia* which means "unveiling," to uncover that which was hidden, to disclose or reveal what was unknown. In the Word proclaimed, it is Jesus Christ's own Heart that is unveiled to us. The *Catechism of the Catholic Church* quotes St. Thomas Aquinas regarding the connection between the Scriptures and the Heart of Jesus Christ: *The phrase "heart of Christ" can refer to Sacred Scripture, which makes known his heart,* (112). Do you know what is in Christ's Heart for you? Do you know who you are to Him? Isaiah speaks the Word of the Lord to Jerusalem—and to us:

> You shall be a glorious crown in the hand of the Lord, a royal diadem held by your God. No more shall men call you "Forsaken," or your land "Desolate," but you shall be called "My Delight," and your land "Espoused." For the Lord delights in you, and makes your land His spouse. As a young man marries a virgin, your Builder shall marry you, and as a bridegroom rejoices in his bride, so shall your God rejoice in you. (Isaiah 62:3–5)

Do you feel forsaken? Do you want to ask God, "Where are You? Are You with me at Mass? I feel so desolate. I feel so cut off—cut off from those I love, from a way out, from a way forward, from a sense of connection with You." If you feel this way, then listen to God's heart for you. You are His *delight.* He wants you to know and *encounter* that truth, to disclose it to you, to uncover what is presently hidden from your sight. This is the Word that awaits us in the unveiling of God's heart.

A tremendous opportunity is presented to you when you sit down to listen to the Readings at Mass. You are present at a moment when Jesus Christ says to you personally, "Sit down. Let me open my heart and share it with you. I will also show you what is in your heart. Do not be afraid." To paraphrase Pope John Paul II, only Jesus Christ can reveal His heart to us and reveal our hearts to ourselves. He pierces through the layers of our confusion, fear, and doubt. He unveils the attitudes, desires and attachments that keep us tied down and He shows us our true desire to love Him with all our heart and soul. That is why this part of the Mass is such a drama. Will we be attentive? As the Readings are proclaimed, will we be open and alert to the unveiling of the heart of Christ for us, as well as the unveiling of our hearts to ourselves?

THANKS BE TO GOD

Notice we don't get to pick what parts of the Bible are proclaimed to us. We don't get to choose what "Word of the Lord" is read at Mass. Our job is to be open to whatever Word our Lord would speak to us, whether it be comforting and consoling, or convicting and challenging. No matter what the Word proclaimed in the First and Second Readings, our response is always the same:

"Thanks be to God!" When Jesus reveals how much He loves you, your response is "Thanks be to God!" When Jesus speaks a Word that shows you how deeply you are mired in sin and you face His judgment, your response is still the same, "Thanks be to God!"

THE RESPONSORIAL PSALM

As the Lord speaks to us in His Word, we are called upon to respond, not just as a community, but personally. The Word that the Lord speaks is spoken to *me*. How can I respond appropriately? The Responsorial Psalm comes between the First and Second Readings. It offers me a way to personally respond to the Word of God just proclaimed, but in a way that doesn't remove me from the community. How? By praying a first person "I" prayer along with many other "I's". Responsorial Psalms are almost always first person prayers. They use "I" and "me." I don't have to make up my own response, the Psalm equips me with a Word *from* God to speak *to* God. The Psalms inspire me to respond, "The Lord is my light and my salvation; whom do I fear? ... One thing I ask of the Lord, this I seek, to dwell in the house of the Lord all the days of my life" (Psalm 27). "In you, Lord, I take refuge; let me never be put to shame" (Psalm 31).

Did you ever notice that sometimes the Responsorial Psalm asks you to say or sing a response that is not at all reflective of how you're feeling that Sunday? For instance, it says:

> To you, LORD, I call; my Rock do not be deaf to me. If you fail to answer me, I will join those who go down to the pit.
> Hear the sound of my pleading when I cry to you, lifting my hands toward your holy place.
> (Psalm 28)

This is someone who is in desperate straits, and frankly, when I go to Mass, I'm rarely feeling like that! And yet I am asked to pray a Psalm that puts me in the place of one who is in that condition. Why? Because I am part of the Body of Christ, the Church. St. Paul tells us we are "individually parts of one another" (Romans 12:5) and that we therefore should "Rejoice with those who rejoice, weep with those who weep" (Romans 12:15). In short, even though the Responsorial Psalm emphasizes my personal response to the Word of the Lord, sometimes the actual response I am praying stretches me beyond my own current situation, and asks me to join with others in the Church who are in that condition. This frees me from being overly focused on how I am feeling right now, and invites me to be drawn into the lives of those around me. So the Responsorial Psalm will always be a fitting prayer even if it doesn't always fit with my personal situation. Sometimes I pray it vigorously because it reflects my situation. Other times, I pray it with a sense of solidarity or compassion when it doesn't fit my situation but does fit the situation of others in the Body of Christ.

STANDING FOR CHRIST

After the Second Reading, we have the Gospel. The first thing that happens is that we all stand up. Why do we do stand at the time of the Gospel? It is not a strategy devised to help get the blood flowing again after sitting for so long. Then why stand?

I'm sure you've seen television shows or movies involving courtroom scenes. Just before the judge enters, the bailiff says, "All rise." Standing is how people appropriately respond when they recognize that the judge is entering the courtroom. Standing is a way of expressing respect for the person of the judge because of the office he holds. Similarly, we stand up at the reading of the Gospel because it is our appropriate response to the presence of Jesus Christ *Who is proclaimed* in every Gospel and *Who proclaims* every Gospel. Jesus Christ proclaims His Gospel. We stand as a sign of our reverence for our Lord. This sheds some light on why the reading of the Gospel is reserved for those who are ordained. The ordained minister is one consecrated to Jesus Christ the High Priest in a special way through the sacrament of Holy Orders. He is an ordained mouthpiece for the Lord at the proclamation of the Gospel.

When the Gospel is read we make the sign of the cross on our forehead, lips, and hearts. In doing that we are saying we intend to dedicate or consecrate our mind, our speech (our words) and our hearts—the very center of our being, our lives—to Jesus Christ and His Gospel. By repeating this simple gesture, we are saying, "I believe Your teaching. I will speak Your word. I will follow You. I give You my life. My life is dedicated to Your Gospel. You have the words of everlasting life." Notice one more thing: we make the sign of the cross on our foreheads, lips and over our hearts before the Gospel is proclaimed. We stand and announce to the Lord that we will believe whatever He is going to teach us in this Gospel *before* we hear it. Sometimes His message is not easy to speak or to receive, yet we signify that our hearts are open and our lives are dedicated to receive and proclaim it. That is the gesture of radical faith in the Lord that we make at every Mass.

In Genesis 21, when the Lord called him by name, Abraham responded with a one word answer, "Ready!" before he knew what the Lord was going to ask of him. Our gesture of making the sign of the cross on our foreheads, lips and over our hearts is a way of saying to the Lord that we are ready to believe, ready to speak and ready to live out what the Lord is about to proclaim to us in this Gospel. When Abraham answered "Ready," he was asked by the Lord to take his only son, the son he loved, to a place where he would offer his life in sacrifice.

I wonder, as Abraham walked with Isaac whether he wished he had responded differently when God called out to him? I wonder if he wished he'd said, "What?" Of course, Abraham's response was an expression of tremendous trust in the Lord. As we stand and hear the Gospel, the sign of the cross we make can signal our trust in and entrustment to the Lord. The gesture of signing ourselves is dramatic. What are we saying to the Lord as we stand to hear His Gospel? Are we saying "What?" or "Ready!"

GOD'S IDEAS, NOT GOOD IDEAS

After the Gospel we sit again and the priest delivers a homily. It is profoundly enriching to realize the mission of the homilist, especially because we might easily assume that the homilist is more or less just somebody whose job is to talk. The reality is that the homilist is the one whose ears are even more important than his mouth. He is the one who needs to have a greater capacity to hear than to speak. Why? Because it's the mission of the homilist to discern the answer to the following question, "God, what is your message for your people?" The homily is not the opportunity for the priest or deacon to come up with his own ideas, as good as they might be. The homilist is like an angel. He is to bring God's message, not his, to God's people. How would you like to have the responsibility of carrying out that mission? Can you imagine reading the Scriptures for Sunday, then going to pray and asking

God, "What is the message You want me to speak to Your people?" and then discerning a way to deliver that message? Being a homilist is an amazing call. If we really knew what was at stake in a homily, we would be a lot more merciful towards our priests and deacons!

Sometimes we settle for the attitude of the critic. We sit there saying inside ourselves, "All right, Father, I expect you to make this interesting and relevant. Don't forget to include a dash of humor and, oh yeah, make it applicable to my life. And make sure you keep it under nine minutes." Then as we listen we can be quick to say, "Why did he say that? I would have said it this way," or "I would have made a different point." If we could only remember that the Lord Jesus Himself is present during the *Liturgy of the Word*. He has a Word that is just for you; it is in His heart, and during this particular Mass He intends to speak it to you. One way He intends to accomplish this is through His ordained mouthpiece. He intends to use the priest's or deacon's homily as a conduit for communicating His word to you.

It is not God's fault if we are present at Mass but fail to hear the Lord speak when the Gospel is proclaimed and when the homily is given. Some of you may be thinking, "I have a less than inspiring or less than orthodox priest at my parish. What is God saying?" To my mind it's quite simple. God is speaking a very loud message: pray for your priest. Pray for your deacon. You are to pray for your priest that he may have ears to hear. And pray that you may have ears to hear. Trust me. The Lord will work with and through your priest's words or He will work around and despite them. God's Word is not stopped so easily unless we are stopping up our ears and refusing to listen. Don't allow a homilist's failures, even his sins against preaching the Word well, to constitute an excuse for your refusal to listen well to the Word.

THE CREED

After the homily we are again invited to stand and, in fact, *to take a stand* for what we believe by praying the Creed. What is the Creed? It is the Church's profession of faith. It is the Church taking a stand on the meaning of it all. We are boldly proclaiming what we believe regarding the most profound and important realities in life. Not because we have figured it all out, but because God has revealed the truth of these matters. We are taking a stand about what this world is about, Who God is, Who Christ is, what our situation in life is, where this world is headed, and what realities God has placed on this earth to draw us to Himself. God's truth is proclaimed by us in the Creed, and by standing and reciting it we announce "Here is where I stand about what matters most in the world."

This Creed was handed over to me in baptism. Catechumens, those who enter the Catholic Church as adults, go through a special rite where the Creed is handed over to them. It is a special entrustment of a gift from Heaven. But the handing over is a two-way street. Not only does the Church hand over the Creed to us, we hand ourselves over to the Creed. In receiving the Creed, I am welcoming all that the Creed says to me as the Truth about the meaning of my life and of everyone's life. This Truth needs witnesses. This Truth needs people to take a stand and profess it with their lips and with their lives. At Mass, we profess it together with our lips. Hopefully, we do so with an awareness of the meaning of what we are saying. We are taking a stand and professing before God and the world, that this is the Truth which shapes how we live and if necessary, how we die. Not something to be taken lightly or spoken mindlessly!

PRAYING WITH THE ANGELS AND SAINTS

After the Creed, we offer the *Prayers of the Faithful*. I would like to share three insights that help me enter this part of the Mass much more deeply than I otherwise would. Hopefully they will encourage you to a more profound understanding of intercessory prayer, thus helping you recognize and respond to what's at stake at Mass in this moment.

First, if we focus on the idea that we are at Mass to give thanks and praise to God, then praying for others during Mass might feel a bit out of place. What helps here is remembering that we are drawn into the reality of Heaven during Mass. What is Jesus Christ, our High Priest, doing in Heaven? To be sure, Jesus Christ, God and man, leads us in our praise and thanks to the Father. But the Scriptures say Jesus is also doing something else; He is interceding for us on earth. So are the angels and saints. Our *Prayers of the Faithful* can be seen as another indication that we on earth are drawn into the reality of Heaven. Our intercessory prayers are caught up into those of the saints, angels and ultimately of Christ Himself, the One Intercessor with the Father. As my awareness of that grew, my desire to be more focused and alert grew tremendously.

INTERCESSORY PRAYER: GOD'S ATTEMPT TO GET US INVOLVED

Second, the Word of God makes it clear that God wants us to ask for good things from Him. Right in the midst of our celebration of praise and worship of God, when we are expressing most fully who we are, the Lord commands and invites us to ask Him for good things. When we pray for ourselves, we pray a prayer of petition. When we pray for others, it is called intercessory prayer. Often, I hear Catholics talk about intercessory prayer in a way that is completely backwards, as if it is our attempt to get God to notice some situation He hasn't seen and to get Him to do something that He hasn't considered. It sounds something like this: "God, Betty is in the hospital and is very sick. Would you please help her get better right away? She really needs to get better soon. Her family needs her to be well."

Intercessory prayer is not our attempt to get God to notice a situation. Still less is it about our recommending a course of action to a God who needs our advice. Intercessory prayer is God's attempt to get us involved in bringing about the blessing that He intends to give. Please read that again. God intends to bless the situation, but He graciously and mysteriously chooses to do it through us. That is why Pascal said, "God has instituted prayer to lend human beings the dignity of being causes." God draws us to pray for situations He intends to bless through us. Our intercessory prayers make us collaborators with Him, fulfilling our part, so that God is freed to bless us and the world in the way that He is waiting and willing and wanting to do.

That raises the question, if intercessory prayer is our responding to God's willingness to bless situations, then why do we have to pray for so long for Him to actually send that blessing? There isn't a simple answer to the question, but I have gleaned an important insight from our tradition. St. Augustine teaches that prayer is essentially desire or yearning. When we pray and our prayers are not answered, we will continue to yearn in prayer. Through our persevering, pleading in prayer and begging God to bless someone, we are being stretched. That is a blessing all by itself. In addition, our yearning calls for grace to increasingly be released into that person's life, and the capacity of the person we are interceding for begins to stretch. Eventually, they will be stretched sufficiently to receive the blessing that God was always ready to give. They simply weren't able to contain it. This is a fundamental reason why Jesus urges us to be "importunate" in prayer. We persist in prayer, not because God is deaf, but because we need to grow or the situation we are praying for needs to be stretched large enough to receive all that God is waiting to give.

Of course, we will sometimes find that the blessing we seek is not the one God wants to give. But if we are open in our intercessory prayer we will be led beyond what we were initially asking for to what the Lord actually desires to give in that situation. When we recognize that the *Prayers of the Faithful* are an opportunity for us to be God's collaborators in bringing about His plan to bless the situations we lift up to Him, we will engage in this part of the Mass with much more fervor.

LIVING ON BEHALF OF OTHERS

I mentioned earlier that there were three insights that helped me pray the *Prayers of the Faithful* with greater liveliness. The third insight is a principle that goes right down to the roots of revelation: the mysterious fact that the Chosen are chosen for the sake of the Unchosen. It's a fact we see again and again in Scripture. Abraham is chosen by God out of all the nations of the world. But before we can complain that this is unfair, we discover why: so that all the nations of the earth will be blessed through him. Israel is made a priestly people while other peoples are not. Why? So that Israel can be a light to the Gentiles. Christ is the Chosen One, so that in Him all those who were without hope and without God in the world might be chosen too!

The privilege of being at Mass is not a blessing that is intended just for me. The *Prayers of the Faithful* is a moment when we can recognize in a special way that we are at Mass not only for ourselves, but for the sake of and on behalf of those who are not present, who do not even desire to be present, who do not even have a clue that the Lord is longing to bless them. The *Prayers of the Faithful* are an opportunity to be a voice for the "unfaithful"; we are present for those who are absent. Do you ever wonder, "Why do I maintain my Catholic faith when my brother has fallen away, when my sister no longer attends, when my parents no longer believe, when my kids no longer practice? Why have I been so blessed to love my Catholic faith?" Here is my answer: I have absolutely no idea. I do know, however, that because you are at Mass, you are not there only for yourself. During the *Prayers of the Faithful* you can stand for all of your family members, friends, and loved ones who are not there. Pray on their behalf. Pray for their sake. In the mystery of God's plan, they are not where you are and you are not where they are. You are not to judge why that is. You are to pray that they may all one day be with you. In the meantime, they are with you, in your heart as you stand before God on their behalf. Lord, hear our prayer!

CHAPTER FOUR

JESUS CHRIST PRESENT IN THE PRIEST

Although failure to observe the pascal solemnity would be very grave offense, it would be still more dangerous to take part in the liturgy without sharing in our Lord's passion ... We can give authentic worship to the suffering, dead, and risen Christ only if we ourselves suffer, die, and rise again with him.

Pope St. Leo the Great

WELCOMING THE CROSS

There is something about the Cross that a Catholic should not want to escape. Even though I'm not a priest, I did spend five years discerning that vocation in the seminary. One evening we were watching a video given by a seminarian's parents. The video was on a VHS tape, back in the day before DVDs. The movie had been recorded off the television onto what was originally a blank videotape. However, this wasn't the first movie recorded on the tape. The movie we were watching had been recorded over another movie. Part way into the film, I realized that it was what I called a borderline movie; it came perilously close to the point where seminarians (or any Christian gentleman) should probably not be watching. When a questionable scene occurred, everyone got very quiet and still. The unspoken decision we were all making was to let the scene pass and hope that nothing worse would show up later in the movie.

It went along like this for a good bit of the movie when suddenly the screen image started to break up and the film it had been taped over broke through. Lo and behold, the movie that had been taped over was *Jesus of Nazareth*. And the exact part of the movie that showed up was the scene of Jesus being scourged at the pillar. As each brutal blow was delivered, the chains that bound Jesus' hands to the pillar rattled. We were stunned into a different kind of silence by the intense scene. This lasted for about five seconds and then that image broke up and the other movie we were watching re-emerged on the screen. You can imagine what happened next. It took less than a minute for the lights to come on, the movie to be turned off, and all the seminarians to leave the room chastened and saddened.

This true story points out in dramatic fashion the concrete difference that Christ's Passion and death makes when it breaks into the events of our lives. What a gift we seminarians received when the Cross of Christ suddenly broke through. It shined a particularly bright light onto our activity of watching a movie we all knew we should have turned off. When we were able to link our present activity to Christ's Passion and death, we were changed.

What if Jesus' Passion, death and Resurrection could break through into our lives today? What if Christ's redeeming death could be brought near to us? What if that event, which happened two thousand years ago was able to break into today in a real and meaningful way? The astonishing news is that it not only can, but it does. At Mass. Yes, that's what we believe. Jesus' Paschal Mystery is not trapped in the past as a fixed event. At Mass, the Paschal Mystery is made present to us. If you've been following me through the Mass to this point, your vision just got stretched in another direction. At Mass, not only does Heaven break into earth, which is incredible enough all by itself, but the past breaks into the present. Not just any old part of the past, but the happenings involving Jesus Christ's Passion, death, Resurrection and Ascension. These events are all incorporated into that singular event called the Paschal Mystery. This is what is breaking into our midst at Mass.

The in-breaking of the movie *Jesus of Nazareth* had a big impact on us as movie watchers. Imagine the impact if we were aware that going to Mass involved being present and participating in the ritual where the actual event of Jesus Christ's Paschal Mystery broke through! What if we could have some kind of living encounter with the event of Jesus Christ's death on Calvary and Resurrection from the dead? It would change our lives ... and so it will, if only we have eyes to see, ears to hear and respond well.

Before we explore that, let's ask the question, how is it possible for these past events to break into our present at Mass? It can and does happen because Jesus Himself, Who is not only man but God, established that it would happen like this. When did He do that? At the Last Supper. The *Catechism of the Catholic Church* explains it this way:

> In the liturgy of the Church [i.e. at Mass], it is principally his own Paschal mystery that Christ signifies and makes present. During his earthly life Jesus announced his Paschal mystery by his teaching and anticipated it by his actions. When his Hour comes, he lives out the unique event of history which does not pass away: Jesus dies, is buried, rises from the dead, and is seated at the right hand of the Father "once for all." His Paschal mystery is a real event that occurred in our history, but it

is unique: all other historical events happen once, and then they pass away, swallowed up in the past. The Paschal mystery of Christ, by contrast, cannot remain only in the past, because by his death he destroyed death, and all that Christ is—all that he did and suffered for all men—participates in the divine eternity, and so transcends all times while being made present in them all. The event of the Cross and Resurrection *abides* and draws everything toward life. (1085)

Don't worry if you find that passage from the Catechism to be difficult to understand. It *is* difficult to understand. In fact, we will never fully comprehend it precisely because it is a mystery. That means it's too big for our finite minds to contain. It overflows on every side. The Paschal Mystery is, however, a reality that we can welcome into our lives and encounter in a life-changing way at Mass. Why? Because of Jesus Christ's presence in the priest.

If it's true that the ritual of the Mass puts us into life-changing contact with the Paschal Mystery, it's Jesus Christ's presence in the priest that makes this possible. Jesus Christ is present in the priest in a distinctive way because of what happens to a man when he receives the sacrament of Holy Orders. A priest is ordained to be an *alter Christus,* "another Christ." By the power of the Holy Spirit, the priest makes Jesus' own sacrifice on the Cross present at Mass. Let's see how this shows up as we move through the Mass.

PRESENTING OURSELVES AS A PRESENT

In the last chapter, we walked through the *Liturgy of the Word,* ending with the *Prayers of the Faithful.* Once those are completed, we sit once again and begin the second major part of the Mass, *The Liturgy of the Eucharist.* This begins with what is called the *Presentation of the Gifts,* when the *Gifts*—the bread and the wine (and the collection)—are brought to the altar, ordinarily from the back of the Church.

The *Presentation of the Gifts* involves a family, couple or other representatives from the congregation carrying the bread, wine and collection basket up to the priest and handing them off. It seems like such a minor activity that it wouldn't be specially identified in the ritual of the Mass. Yet it is. In fact, for me personally, it is one of the most dramatic parts of the Mass for us in the pews. It is a moment when we can be acutely aware that the pew is on the playing field. We are in the game. We are participants. Why? Because of the meaning of walking up and handing over the bread and wine to the priest. What does this handing over mean? It signifies our handing our lives over to God!

If you grew up Catholic, your first inclination is to think that the bread and wine at Mass represent the body and blood of Jesus Christ. If we were just a little bit further into the ritual of the Mass, you would be right. The bread and wine handed over to the priest in the *Presentation of the Gifts* will represent (as in "make present") Jesus Christ. But not yet. Not at this point in the Mass. Before they re-present the body and blood of Jesus Christ at Mass the bread and wine, these gifts, represent (as in "stand for" or "symbolize") you and me. They represent our lives offered as a "spiritual sacrifice." That is why the bread and wine are brought forth from the midst of the community by members of the community. The bread and wine stand for you and me and everyone else in the church.

Think about that for a moment. It is your life that is being put into the hands of the priest: your past, present, and future; your hopes and dreams; your family and friends; your loves, hates, and fears; your difficulties and joys, hurts and pains. All that you are and have is being freely given over to God in the symbolic gesture of presenting the bread and wine into the hands of the priest, in whom there is a special presence of Jesus Christ the High Priest. That is the meaning of the gesture of the *Presentation of the Gifts,* but understanding the gesture isn't the most important thing. The most important thing is that this gesture corresponds to what is actually happening in your mind and heart at this moment in the Mass. Are you a willing "sacrifice"?

OFFERING OURSELVES IN SACRIFICE

Sacrifice? That doesn't sound so good. After all, what happens to sacrificial goats, sheep and cattle in the Bible? They are killed. Or in more contemporary terms, when we think of making a sacrifice, we think of giving something up that we'd rather keep. The idea of giving something up helps shed some light on what it means that the bread and wine are offered to God as a spiritual sacrifice.

The word "sacrifice" comes from two Latin words which literally mean "to make holy." To make something holy means to take it out of ordinary usage and set it apart for God's purpose. In the Old Testament, it meant that the animal brought to the Jewish priest to be sacrificed or "made holy" no longer belonged to its owner; it belonged to God, it became God's property. The lamb is no longer part of the flock; it is given up to God and set apart for His purpose. Indeed, it is *killed*; it is set apart so radically that there is no way it can be brought back into the flock. There is no returning it back to its pre-sacrificial condition.

GOING "ALL IN"

We'll be focusing on how the Mass connects us to Jesus' Sacrifice on the Cross in just a moment. But before we reach that point in the Mass, stop and reflect with me on what is happening when the priest receives the gifts of bread and wine (remember, that means you!) He approaches the *altar* with these gifts. Yes, what you put into the hands of the priest is to be "sacrificed." In this moment, you are being "made holy" by being "offered up in sacrifice." You are being taken out of an ordinary life (where your life is your own to do with as you please) and you are set apart for God's purpose and plan for your life. You no longer belong to yourself.

Have you ever thought about that? At every Mass, during the *Presentation of the Gifts,* you are watching a gesture that expresses that you belong to God. You are His. "You are not your own. You have been purchased, and at a price" (1 Corinthians 6:19–20). You are "made holy." That means you are no ordinary person. There is no such thing as an ordinary person at Mass. There are only people who have been drawn out of ordinary ways of seeing who they are, what their life is about, what their past is, and where they are going. You are now set apart for God's purpose for your life. You are God's special possession.

That is what we are invited to recognize and freely do at Mass—whether we realize it or not. If we have eyes to see, we see that we are invited to give it all. And here is the drama of the moment: as that bread and wine are brought to the priest, ask yourself if you are a willing participant. You are asked to hold nothing back; no situation, no relationship, no part of your life, all that you are and have, completely, totally, forever handed over to God. The Lord is calling you to be "all in" as they say in Texas Hold 'Em. Hold nothing back. Push all your chips on the table. No bluffing allowed! To go to Mass is to face this dramatic moment when God calls you to be "all in" for His purpose for your life, to give yourself to Him once again.

Once the bread and wine are handed to the priest, he brings them to the altar and offers them to God. We respond to his action by saying "Blessed be God forever!" We are at the altar and we have our first offering! What is the sacrifice the priest offers on this altar? Right now, at this point, it's you and me symbolized by the bread and wine! We were joined to Christ in baptism precisely so that we could *offer our bodies as a living sacrifice, holy and acceptable to God, our spiritual worship* (Romans 12:1). If this hasn't been clear to us, it's not because the concept that we are offering a spiritual sacrifice has been hidden. It is right in front of us in the "dialogue" the priest has with us at this very moment in the Mass. He reminds us that this action is a sacrifice. "Pray, my brothers and sisters, that *our sacrifice* may be acceptable to God, the almighty Father." Our response to the priest's invitation confirms that we aware that we are offering a sacrifice: "May the Lord accept *the sacrifice* at your hands, for the praise and glory of his name, for our good and for the good of all his church."

In Chapter One, I focused on the fact that the Mass is a time for "Eucharist"—a time to thank and praise God in a way that He deserves. I wrote about paying the debt of gratitude to God we feel in our hearts. At this moment, we are shown what it's going to cost us to give God the praise and thanks He is due. Do you really want to offer God fitting thanks and praise? Do you want to pay that debt of gratitude? If you do, know what it is going to cost you. It is going to cost you nothing less than *everything*—exactly what it cost Jesus Christ in whom our self-offering finds its origin, support and fulfillment.

POURING OUT AND POURING IN

The *Presentation of the Gifts* is our moment of offering ourselves as a "spiritual sacrifice," but this should never be seen in isolation from what Jesus Christ did by offering Himself on the cross. There is a ritual performed by the priest during this part of the Mass that I'd like to focus on in this context. It occurs between the offering of the bread and the offering of the wine. Did you ever notice that the priest pours a little water into the chalice filled with wine? We rarely hear aloud what the priest says, but it is an incredible statement: "By the mystery of this water and wine may we come to share in the divinity of Christ, who humbled Himself to share in our humanity." The historical reason for the gesture of mixing a small amount of water into the wine was that the wine was strong. It was a way of weakening the strength of the wine, by watering it down. But this gesture came to take on a spiritual meaning as well: the wine is the divinity of Christ, and we are the water. It is as if our spiritual self-offering (our "pouring out") at Mass, represented by tasteless, colorless water, is immersed in the robust, flavorful wine of Christ's self-offering on the Cross. What happens to the water when it's poured into the wine? It is totally dissolved into the wine and "becomes wine." That what happens at Mass: our self-offering is going to be immersed into Christ's.

We are actually getting a little hint here into where Mass is headed. Do you know what is happening to our humanity through this giving over of our lives as a "spiritual sacrifice"? Our humanity is being "mixed" with the divinity of Jesus. If you've ever thought yourself of no account or little importance, surrender that notion! You are no longer just a human being. Your life, just as you are, is immersed in the very divine life of Christ at Mass. St. Peter tells us that we "become sharers in the divine nature" (2 Peter 1:4). If we recognized this is what happens at every Mass, that we are asked to be all in, and that a deeper share in God's own divine nature was the result, would we even be able to contain our astonishment? How could anyone possibly be bored when these are the stakes?

THE HEART OF THE PRIESTHOOD

Now after the priest offers our gifts as a spiritual sacrifice, the priest has a dialogue with us that will lead us to the heart of the Mass, called the Eucharistic Prayer or *Canon of the Mass:*

> Priest: The Lord be with you.
> Us: And also with you.
> Priest: Lift up your hearts.
> Us: We lift them up to the Lord.
> Priest: Let us give thanks to the Lord our God.
> Us: It is right to give him thanks and praise.

Notice the language. It mentions the heart. What is the heart we are lifting up here? Of course, not our physical hearts over which we made a sign of the cross before the Gospel. The heart is the center of who you are, the very core of your being. The priest's invitation to have us lift up our hearts is an invitation to offer ourselves to God, down to the very core of our being, confirming what we just did a moment ago with the bread and wine. While we do these things we stand, signifying by our words and posture that we are actively involved in giving ourselves to God. Why? To give Him thanks and praise. That's why we are at Mass!

During this part of the Mass, Christ's presence in the priest becomes most profoundly expressed. We will see this unfold beginning with what happens next. First, the priest addresses a prayer to God the Father that ends with an invitation to join our voices with those of angels, archangels and the whole company of Heaven and cry out:

Holy, Holy, Holy Lord, God of power and might. Heaven and earth are full of Your glory. Hosanna in the highest Blessed is He who comes in the name of the Lord. Hosanna in the highest!

This prayer is called the *Sanctus*, which means "Holy." Where do the words of the prayer come from? Two places: Heaven and earth. The beginning of this prayer comes from a heavenly vision granted to the prophet Isaiah:

In the year King Uzziah died, I saw the Lord seated on a high and lofty throne, with the train of his garment filling the temple. Seraphim were stationed above; each of them had six wings: with two they veiled their faces, with two they veiled their feet, and with two they hovered aloft. "Holy, holy, holy is the LORD of hosts!" they cried one to the other. "All the earth is filled with his glory!" (Isaiah 6:1–3)

By putting a prayer from a biblical vision of heavenly worship on our lips, we are asked to recognize that our prayers at Mass draw us up into the worship of God in Heaven. Once again we bump up against a need to listen to what we've been hearing and saying as Catholics and realize the implications. If the typical manner of our saying or singing the *Sanctus* is any measure of our recognition of where we are at Mass, then we have a long way to go.

The second half of the *Sanctus* comes from Jesus' triumphal entry into Jerusalem on Palm Sunday. Crying out "Blessed is He who comes in the name of the Lord" was a way of announcing that the Son of David, the Messiah, was coming to inaugurate His kingdom in His holy city. There is one big surprise. Jesus chose to enter the city in a humble way, riding on a donkey. The Church invites us to make these words our own at this point in the Mass. Why? Because Jesus Christ is about to enter His holy place in a humble way. He is coming as what looks like bread and wine. We respond to this recognition of His humble arrival by humbling ourselves before what is about to happen. We do this by kneeling.

OUR RADICAL INTERDEPENDENCE

We come at last to the very high point of the Mass where two very dramatic elements occur. They are what the ritual calls the *Epiclesis* and the *Prayer of Consecration.* The *Epiclesis* is that part of the Mass where the priest puts his hands over the bread and wine—which up to this point symbolized us—and calls down the Holy Spirit so that they will be transformed into the Body and Blood of Jesus Christ.

It should be noted that the *Epiclesis* does not stand alone. In order to go from bread and wine to the Real Presence of Jesus Christ, body, blood, soul and divinity, we have another action: the *Prayer of Consecration.* The

Prayer of Consecration is when the priest repeats the words of Jesus at the Last Supper, "Take this all of you and eat it ..."

Please notice four vital things: first, the priest must call down the Holy Spirit before he can take up Jesus' part in the Last Supper and pray the *Prayer of Consecration*. On his own, the priest does not have the ability to turn bread and wine into the Real Presence of Jesus Christ, body, blood, soul and divinity. The priest is totally dependent upon the Holy Spirit to bring about this transformation.

The second vital thing to notice is this: The Holy Spirit, who is God Almighty, could, on His own, turn the bread and wine into the body, blood, soul and divinity of Jesus Christ without a priest at all. *But He has willed not to.* God has willed to work through the ordained bishops and priests in whom Jesus Christ the High Priest is present in a special way. By God's sovereign power, there is this mutuality of dependence whereby for the priest to fulfill his call, he absolutely needs the Holy Spirit to come down to bring about this transformation. And for the Holy Spirit to bring about what He wills, He has willed to need an ordained bishop or priest.

Third, this radical mutual interdependence between the Holy Spirit and the priest at this point in the Mass shines a light on a similar reality in our lives as disciples of Jesus Christ. Just as God has a purpose for the priest's life, so it is true that God has a purpose for your life. At the same time, just as the priest is absolutely dependent on God to work the miraculous transformation of the bread and wine into the body and blood of Christ, so it is also absolutely true that you have no power to fulfill *your* God-given purpose without Him.

Fourth, just as God has chosen not to give us the Eucharist except through the hands of His priests, so God has a work that He wants to accomplish in and through you. It is true that if you do not do the work that He wants to accomplish through you, He might choose to accomplish it in some other way. Nevertheless it is just as true that there are things you are called to do. You have been given gifts for the upbuilding of the Church, and you have been brought into contact with people with whom God intends you to share your faith. It is no accident you were born in this moment in the place where you are. God made you to do what must be done for His kingdom. Right now! Right here! However, He needs you to cooperate with Him to bring about the work He wants to do *in you and through you.* The Holy Spirit needs your "yes" so you can be transformed in the way that He intends for you to be. This incredible mutuality of dependence shows up in the Mass, and reflects what is also true in our lives.

STANDING IN CHRIST'S PLACE

In the *Prayer of Consecration* the priest takes up the bread and the wine and says:

On the night he was betrayed, he took bread and gave you thanks and praise. He broke the bread, gave it to his disciples, and said:

Take this, all of you, and eat it: this is my body which will be given up for you.

When supper was ended, he took the cup. Again he gave you thanks and praise, gave the cup to his disciples, and said:

Take this, all of you, and drink from it: this is the cup of my blood, the blood of the new and everlasting covenant. It will be shed for you and for all so that sins may be forgiven. Do this in memory of me.

Fr. Robert Sokolowski in his amazing book, *Eucharistic Presence,* points out that there is an important shift in the *Eucharistic Prayer,* a shift from narration to quotation. The priest shifts from telling the story in third person, "He took bread and gave you thanks ..." *to quoting in first person,* "Take this, all of you and eat it, this is My body ... Take this all of you, and drink from it: this is the cup of My blood." Why is this significant? Because during the *Prayer of Consecration,* he is allowing Jesus Christ the High Priest, present in him, to speak. The priest is acting *in persona Christi capitis,* in the person of Christ the Head. In so doing, we are able to encounter for ourselves, the Paschal Mystery of Jesus Christ's Passion, death and Resurrection.

In *Eucharistic Presence,* Fr. Sokolowski notes that at the Last Supper, Jesus prophetically anticipates His death on the cross by His taking up bread and wine and saying, "This is My body... This is My blood... given for you." There is a great example of what this means in the movie *The Passion of the Christ.* In that movie, we see a cinematic attempt to relate Jesus' Last Supper with His death on Calvary. For instance, when Jesus takes the cloth off of the basket of bread, the camera immediately cuts to Jesus being stripped of His cloak on Calvary. When Jesus lifts up the bread at the Last Supper saying, "Take this and eat it," the movie cuts to the crucifix being lifted up on Calvary. The film powerfully illustrates the idea that Jesus, at the Last Supper, is prophetically anticipating what will happen a mere eighteen hours later.

What about us? We don't celebrate Mass hours before but rather 2,000 years after the Crucifixion of Jesus. Sokolowski points out that what Jesus prophetically *anticipates,* we *remember.* But the word remember is misleading for us. When we remember, we call to mind an event that is past and stays in the past, except in our minds. That is not the biblical meaning of remembering. The word in Greek for remembering is *anamnesis.* To remember, for the Jewish mind, was to make present, really and effectively. It is through an established ritual that the remembering of an event occurred.

As an example, consider the Exodus, when the Hebrews were delivered from slavery in Egypt. In Exodus 12, God tells the Jewish people how they should ritually remember this event every year in the Passover, which is to be a "perpetual memorial." Scripture declares that all future generations of Israel are to repeat this ritual dialogue:

> When your children ask you, "What does this rite of yours mean?" you shall reply, "This is the Passover sacrifice of the LORD, who passed over the houses of the Israelites in Egypt; when he struck down the Egyptians, he spared our houses." (Exodus 12:26–27)

Note that they say "our" houses. Children centuries later speak of the Exodus as though they were personally present. The Passover rite "makes present" the events of the Exodus to Jews separated by five millennia and half a world away from the events recorded in the book of Exodus. It doesn't say, "Our ancestors were slaves in Egypt" but "we" were slaves in Egypt. Through the ritual, they share in the events remembered.

The same idea is at work in Joshua 24 when Joshua renews the covenant upon Israel's entry into the Promised Land. Recall that the whole generation of the Exodus has died and Joshua is now addressing the generation born after the deliverance from Egypt. Nobody hearing Joshua

speaking experienced even a day of slavery in Egypt. Yet
God addresses them through Joshua:

> Then I sent Moses and Aaron, and smote
> Egypt with the prodigies which I wrought in her
> midst. Afterward, I led you out of Egypt, and when
> you reached the sea, the Egyptians pursued your
> fathers to the Red Sea with chariots and horsemen.
> Because they cried out to the Lord, he put dark-
> ness between your people and the Egyptians, upon
> whom He brought the sea, so that it engulfed them.
> After you witnessed what I did to Egypt, and dwelt
> a long time in the desert. (Joshua 24:5–8)

Note the language: you, your fathers, you. It was their
fathers who witnessed it, but as part of God's people, the
Israelites are being brought back into the very realities
that are symbolized in the covenant ritual. These realities
are "remembered"—they are made truly and effectively
present.

The point is this: the same thing happens at Mass!
Here too we "remember" Christ's saving Passion, death
and Resurrection in a way that is not merely recalling in
our minds something that happened a long time ago on
the other side of the earth to strangers speaking a dead
language. Rather, this saving reality is made present and
effective to us today. That's what "Do this in memory of
me" means.

ONLY BY GRACE

Do you see the drama the Mass involves us in? When Jesus died on the cross, He didn't die just for the people who had lived up to that point. He died for the sins of all of the people who would ever live. All of the sins that anyone will ever commit in all of history are loaded onto the shoulders of Jesus Christ the Son of God, and He bears them for all. For us. When we choose to sin today, it affects what Jesus suffered 2,000 years ago.

Our present ability to affect the severity of Christ's Passion through our sins was a motivation for some saints to long for death. Of course, their desire to die was a longing to be with the One who was their reason for living. But they also wanted to die to make it impossible for them ever to sin again. They did not want to press that thorn any more fully into His head, scourge Him with more lashes, or allow the darkness, fear and confusion He endured to be any more profound.

Jesus once asked His disciples, "Can you drink the cup I drink?" If we are honest with ourselves, we have to face the fact that, on our own, we can't. By ourselves, we can't be "all in" when it comes to giving ourselves to God in total self-sacrifice as Jesus does. Jesus, after the Last Supper and knowing what was to happen to Him, went to the Mount of Olives singing songs of praise. Could we? How then do we sing such songs at Mass knowing we are not all in, but bluffing? The truth is, the only way that we can possibly be "all in" for Him is through the reality that He is already "all in" for us.

That's what is unveiled in the consecration. Take this, all of you and eat it. This is my body and blood which are given for you. It is as if Jesus is saying to us, "Don't try to make yourself holy enough. I make you holy! I've already died for your sins. Do not carry your sins around; I have already freed you from them! I didn't come for Myself, but for you. I came here to make you a participant in the life I share with My Father and the Holy Spirit. I am here to set you free so that you can show the world what my Risen Life looks like. This is My hour, this liturgy of the Mass, is the summation of My life. And it's all for you, to the glory of My Father!"

That is what happens at Mass. We have displayed before us in Mass the most profound, absolute, perfect commitment of God to us, in love. In very truth, the Mass is the most dramatic thing you will ever be privileged to witness while you breathe. And the fruit of it is genuine spiritual power. Because He is "all in" for me, I can be "all in" for Him. The Mass doesn't just show us who Christ is or talk about what He has done: it communicates that life to us like a million volt charge.

Christ is "all in" because He's holding two aces. I'm all in because I've got nothing and I need His everything. We began the Mass by acknowledging our position before God in the Penitential Rite: "I cannot do this. I'm a sinner.

I can't even want to do this without your help, God. I cannot give myself to You in sacrifice unless You have already given Yourself to me in sacrifice." Now His sacrifice is made present to us through the *Epiclesis* and *Prayer of Consecration*. And by it, He gives me the courage, strength, impetus, confidence, call and power to be "all in" for Him.

LET US PROCLAIM THE MYSTERY OF FAITH

It is because we have received this grace to offer ourselves through Christ's self-offering that we can, in the *Memorial Acclamation*, "proclaim the mystery of faith." This mystery of faith is spoken in several ways. We say, "Christ has died, Christ is risen, Christ will come again." We say, "Lord, by your cross and resurrection, You have set us free. You are the Savior of the world." We say, "Dying, You destroyed our death. Rising, You restored our life. Lord Jesus, come in glory!" Each of these acclamations expresses what we are "memorializing" (making present) at this moment: Jesus Christ's Pascal Mystery.

What is a mystery of faith? In theology, the word mystery means something different than in popular culture. Popularly speaking, a mystery is something that is presently unknown, that will probably one day be known, if we simply think about it hard enough and figure it out. A mystery of faith is different. It is a reality that is so great and so profound, that when it is revealed it overwhelms our ability to know it completely. On the altar, we encounter Jesus Christ in the presence of the priest revealing to us the mystery of His suffering and love for us that is so big, it goes beyond our ability to fully grasp. Indeed, we don't so much grasp it as allow it to grasp us. We are encompassed by this mystery and we stand in awe. And the only thing we can do is cry out, "Christ has died. Christ is risen. Christ will come again." It remains a mystery even as it is unveiled. It's not too dark to see, like a cave. It's too bright to see, like the sun.

THE GREAT AMEN

At the end of the Eucharistic Prayer, the priest lifts up what began as bread and wine but is now changed. In the Catholic tradition this change is called transubstantiation. Transubstantiation means there is a *trans*, a change, in the *substance*. In other words, the very core reality has changed while the accidents, that is, the surface features such as look, taste, feel and smell, remain the same. What does the Eucharist look like? It looks, smells and tastes like bread and wine. But after the *Epiclesis* and the *Prayer of Consecration,* it is no longer bread and wine but the body, blood, soul, and divinity of Jesus Christ. He is really, truly present. That is what is occurring on that altar. We bring ourselves symbolically in the bread and wine. Through the power of the Holy Spirit and Jesus Christ present in the priest, bread and wine are transformed into Jesus Christ.

At this moment, the priest lifts the Host and the chalice containing the Precious Blood, and prays through, with and in Jesus Christ and in "the unity of the Holy Spirit" that "all glory and honor are Yours, Almighty Father, forever and ever." Finally! We give God the glory and the praise and the thanks that are fitting.

To this, we say "the Great Amen." What do we come to do at Mass? We come to give God thanks and praise. That is the meaning of our lives. Why do we put ourselves on the altar as a sacrifice? It is in order to give God thanks and praise. It's also why we work, play, love, sweat, suffer, and, ultimately, die. We lift up our hearts to the Lord, why? To give Him thanks and praise as Christ did. This is going to take all we have. But then we come to realize that we are only able to give thanks and praise because we are linked into the divine praise and glorification of the Father by the Son. If I want to give God thanks and praise for my life, finally I can do it in the way that really gives Him the glory He deserves. I can do it in the way that my heart was made to give. I can do it because I am doing it through, with and in Jesus Christ, who offers His Father perfect worship.

That is what happens at Mass. Christ is present in the community, drawing us up into the very worship of Heaven. Christ is present in the Word, unveiling His heart for us and exposing our hearts to Him, causing us to take up our place in the drama of dramas. Having been welcomed into the praise and worship of God, having heard that Word unveiled, and having been unveiled to God by it, we encounter Christ the High Priest through the ministry of the earthly priest, most profoundly, in the consecration of the Eucharist.

Throughout the Mass, we are faced with a question. Jesus Christ is asking, "Will you be 'all in' or are you just bluffing?" No human being can tell by looking at you. It's between you and Him. In your heart of hearts are you putting yourself, your family, that child of yours, that spouse of yours, into that cup? Are you offering your future? Your present? Your past? Everything? Are you saying to Jesus, "It's all Yours, because You've already shown me that You are all mine. I'm here, because I want to fulfill Your purpose for my life. I need Your strength to do it. And Jesus, let me thank and praise God, finally, in the way that He deserves."

Let's pray that today we have the ears to hear Jesus Christ's question, and respond by being "all in."

CHAPTER FIVE

JESUS CHRIST PRESENT IN THE EUCHARIST

O soul, what then desirest thou?
—Lord, I would see, who thus
  choose Thee.
What fears can yet assail thee now?
—All that I fear is to lose Thee.
Love's whole possession I entreat,
Lord, make my soul Thine own abode,
And I will build a nest so sweet
It may not be too poor for God.

St. Teresa of Avila

NO ORDINARY MASS

What was the most memorable Mass you ever attended? For me, it was the 1989 Easter Vigil, at St. Peter's Basilica in Rome, presided over by Pope John Paul II. Being there was like winning the lottery. Actually, I got to be there because I had won a lottery. The North American College in Rome, where I was a seminarian at the time, had been asked by the Vatican to provide about a dozen seminarians to serve in various roles at the Easter Vigil. Who would get the privilege of serving was determined by picking names out of a hat. Not only was my name selected, but when the liturgical roles were assigned, I was chosen to be the Mitre Bearer, the one who has the task of holding the Pope's hat at those parts of the Mass when he's not wearing it.

Early that Saturday evening, we "chosen ones" walked the short distance to St. Peter's and went inside to the place we were told to gather, at the base of Michelangelo's Pietà. To get there, we passed through a special door which allowed us to get close enough to touch the Pietà and walk all around it. It was probably a once-in-a-lifetime opportunity to see that masterpiece so close up and from unique perspectives. So I took some time to appreciate the beauty of the sculpture from angles inaccessible to most visitors. After a while, the Master of Ceremonies pulled me aside and told me that when the time came to line up for the procession, I and a few others were to go into the Sacristy where the Pope vested, because of our roles at Mass. I decided to go into the Sacristy ahead of schedule and see what was there. Right away I saw the Pope's famous Crozier, his shepherd's staff adorned at the top with St. John of the Cross' rendition of Christ Crucified.

I took hold of the Crozier with both hands and prayed for our Holy Father. Then I saw the pectoral cross that he would be wearing during the Easter vigil, laid out on the counter next to the Pope's vestments. It was an incredible moment. Shortly after that three other seminarians came into the Sacristy with the Master of Ceremonies and another attendant. They lined us up just as an elevator door opened inside the Sacristy itself, and Pope John Paul II appeared! He went down the line and we introduced ourselves to him and had a chance to talk with him briefly. After these introductions the Pope became very focused. What I remember so clearly was him standing before the vesting table and being assisted in the process of vesting for Mass, his eyes locked on the crucifix that was on the wall in front of him. He was absorbed in prayer, gazing on Christ Crucified. Just by watching him, I was drawn into a more prayerful spirit as well.

He led us in a short prayer and then we proceeded out. Outside the Sacristy, all of the other hundred or so people involved in the Procession had been lined up by rank. At the front of the line were the candle bearers, then the lectors, deacons, priests, monsignors, bishops, archbishops, Cardinals, the Pope, and then ... me. As the Mitre Bearer, I was lined up *behind the Pope*. From that vantage point, I was going to witness how people were going to react to the presence of the Pope.

As Mass began, all the lights were off in St. Peter's Basilica and the announcement went out in five languages: "PLEASE, NO USE OF CAMERAS! NO FLASH! NO PHOTOS! NO FLASH!" In the world's major languages these words were repeated and repeated to the immense throng. And do you know what impact that actually had on those waiting for the Pope to appear? None at all. As we processed out, we were greeted by a blinding wall of flashing lights and clicking cameras. I saw in a way I never had before what this man did to people. As he walked by, people were crying and reaching out to him. There was a sense of devotion, of personal affection, of love for this holy man of God who made Jesus Christ so present and real. The magnetism of this man was extraordinary— because his eyes were fixed, not on the flashing lights, but on Christ Crucified.

For three hours I stood on the top step of the high altar, holding the Pope's mitre and praying for the man who wore it. I witnessed people coming up to be Baptized, people coming up to be Confirmed, people coming to receive their first Holy Communion. It was incredible to see folks from around the world, wearing their native dress, approach and kneel before the Pope with tears streaming down their faces as he Baptized or Confirmed them. It filled me with tremendous joy. Joy was the key word describing the Easter Vigil. At the end of Mass, as we processed out, the joy of Easter that filled St. Peter's was palpable. The fifteen thousand people who had crowded into the basilica were spilling out into the piazza in front of St. Peter's. Some were even singing and dancing. Others were dressed all in white, as if in baptismal garments, and they danced in a circle. Christ was risen indeed! I will never forget it.

LEARNING TO SEE AS THE ANGELS SEE

After experiencing a Mass like that, the tendency is to talk as though other Masses are merely *ordinary*. Though some Masses have a way of displaying more majestically, wondrously, and marvelously what is happening on the altar, the fact is that the same Eucharistic miracle makes Christ present at *every* Mass. There is no ordinary Mass. What I saw displayed at that Mass at St. Peter's, the angels see displayed at the most humdrum-looking Mass on a Wednesday morning in St. Anonymous Church in Bugtussle, Oklahoma. That's because, as great as Pope John Paul II was, the Mass was not about him. It was about Jesus. John Paul has gone to his great reward, but Jesus Christ is alive and present on every altar in the world through the Holy Eucharist. So the angels rejoice at every Mass just as I rejoiced that night. Our task is to learn to see with the eyes of the angels and the saints, to see the extraordinary in what appears ordinary.

The goal of this book is to help you see who is present at Mass, Jesus Christ Himself, and to understand how He wants to meet you and change your life. So far we have looked at Christ's presence in the community gathered, Christ's presence in the Word proclaimed, and Christ's presence in the priest who offers sacrifice. The first mode of Christ's presence, in the community, calls us to recognize not only *who* is there at Mass but *where* Mass has brought us. When we come into Mass, we are welcomed into the realm of Heaven. The second mode of Christ's presence, in the Word, invites you to listen to the message God has for you. It's the message you most need to hear. The third mode of Christ's presence, in the priest, invites us to offer a sacrifice of praise in union with the Paschal Mystery of Jesus Christ made present to us.

STRETCHED IN EVERY DIRECTION

Have you noticed that the presences of Christ we have explored to this point take us in unique directions? His presence in the *community* draws us *upwards* from life today into the heavenly realm of eternity; His presence in the *Word* opens us to what comes *down* like lightning from Heaven, striking our lives here, now and today; His presence in the *priest* draws 2,000-year-old events from the *past* into the present. In the community and the Word, there are movements from earth to Heaven and Heaven to earth; from time to eternity and eternity to time. In the priest, we have the past brought into the present. What direction is missing? The *future*. The fourth presence of

Christ, in the Eucharist, draws the dimension of the future into our present moment. Receiving the Holy Eucharist in communion gives us a *foretaste of the heavenly banquet* that awaits us in the *future*. Can you see how much we are stretched at Mass? Jesus Christ's presence at Mass extends our vision in every direction. His presence in the Eucharist will point us towards the future, and point out to us that we are not yet at our true homeland enjoying the heavenly banquet. Let's continue our journey through the Mass to see how this shows up.

GETTING THE COMMUNION RITE RIGHT

We now begin a new part of the Mass called the *Rite of Communion*. Now that Christ is really and truly present in the Eucharist, *the altar becomes a table*. When we think of an altar, we rightly think of a sacrifice. When we think of a table, we think of meal. The Eucharistic Altar is both. That is why we are invited to experience a *communion* with the One who is Holy and then, through Him, with one another. We are invited to a Holy Communion. We who now recognize the Real Presence of Jesus Christ, under the appearance of bread and wine, are to prepare well before we approach the table of the Lord. Communion will involve a more profound encounter with Jesus Christ than we have yet had at Mass. In the Eucharist, He is accessible to the point of being consumable. His power to transform us will never be greater than at the moment of communion. We better get this right.

Let's pay attention to what the *Rite of Communion* has us say and do to prepare for that encounter with Jesus. The first thing to notice is that our prayers and actions express that we are still on the way to our heavenly homeland. Yes, Christ has won the victory, but we are not yet off the battlefield. We are like the Israelites who ritually remember the Exodus in the Passover meal, who approach it as a meal to be eaten "on the way." God instructed the Israelites to celebrate the Passover in this way:

> This is how you are to eat it: with your loins girt, sandals on your feet and your staff in hand, you shall eat like those who are in flight. It is the Passover of the LORD. (Exodus 12:11)

After sharing the first Passover meal, including the Passover Lamb, the Israelites were to be ready to make the journey the Lord had planned for them, a journey leading them out of slavery in Egypt, through the desert and ultimately to the Promised Land. The Passover meal was not about settling and getting comfy in Egypt. It was about being set free to move toward their true home. The Mass, where Christ our Passover Lamb is sacrificed (1 Corinthians 5:7), is similar. Receiving Jesus Christ, the Lamb of God in communion we will experience what the Church calls *a foretaste of Heaven*. But we have far to go; we are not yet home. So the Eucharist is also food for our journey from slavery to sin to the freedom of living as sons and daughters of God.

THE FAMILY THAT PRAYS TOGETHER ...

After the Great Amen, we stand to pray The Our Father. The Our Father or Lord's Prayer is called the perfect prayer because it was taught to us by Jesus Himself. There are several things to notice about this prayer that help us realize that we are still walking on our journey of faith towards God. First, we ask for God's Kingdom to come. What is God's kingdom? The *Catechism of the Catholic Church* teaches that God's Kingdom is where God's kingship reigns:

> In the New Testament, the [Greek] word *basileia* can be translated by "kingship" (abstract noun), "kingdom" (concrete noun) or "reign" (action noun). The Kingdom of God lies ahead of us. It is brought near in the Word incarnate, it is proclaimed throughout the whole Gospel, and it has come in Christ's death and Resurrection. The Kingdom of God has been coming since the Last Supper and, in the Eucharist, it is in our midst. The kingdom will come in glory when Christ hands it over to his Father. (2816)

God's kingdom has come (with the coming of Jesus Christ in our midst 2,000 years ago), is coming (at every Mass, Jesus Christ comes again, especially in the Eucharist), and is to come in all its fullness when Jesus Christ returns in glory. And so we pray "Thy Kingdom come." Lord God, we are desperate for Your Kingdom to break into our world right now and right here! Because the Kingdom is not here in its fullness, the Eucharist is a meal for those of us who are still on the way, like the Passover.

In one of the seven petitions of the Our Father, we ask for something that is particularly Eucharistic: our daily bread. We ask God to feed us every day with bread that is "super-essential" (the literal meaning of the Greek word "daily" according to the *Catechism*). In the Bread from Heaven, Jesus Christ communicates His "super-essential" life to us. Can you see how fitting it is that we pray the Lord's Prayer at this point in the Mass? We are about to receive Jesus Christ, the Bread of Life in communion. Here we are petitioning God for that heavenly gift.

Lastly we pray, "Lead us not into temptation, but deliver us from evil." Significantly, the priest says an additional prayer here: "Deliver us, Lord, from every evil, and grant us peace in our day. In your mercy keep us free from sin and protect us from all anxiety as we wait in joyful hope for the coming of our Savior, Jesus Christ." Who is to be delivered from evil? *We* need to be delivered from evil. Grant us peace when? Grant us peace *in our day*. In other words, we have not yet arrived. This is why the Catholic tradition speaks of man as *homo viator:* one who is on the way. St. Thomas Aquinas says that our fundamental condition on earth is that we are sojourners—people who have not yet arrived. Since we are on the way, we can still fall into evil. We experience temptation and find ourselves in conflict with God, others and our own hearts. We are a Pilgrim People and, like ancient Israel, we are still escaping from the bondage of sin, still learning to be led, still wandering in the desert, still striving to live lives of holiness, still seeking to settle in the Promised Land of Heaven.

We ask God to deliver us. We ask God, in His mercy, to keep us free from sin since, apart from God's mercy, we *will* fall into sin. We ask God to protect us from all anxiety. That's because, when you have not yet arrived, you can become quite anxious. You can start to fear that you might *not* arrive. Or you can become anxious about your loved ones. So we pray that God will free us from all anxiety as we wait in joyful hope for the coming of our Savior Jesus Christ.

... STAYS TOGETHER

After this, the Mass continues with this dialogue:

Priest: The Peace of the Lord be with you always.
Us: And also with you.
Priest: Let us offer each other a sign of peace.

St. Augustine defined peace as *tranquilitas ordinis,* like the untroubled surface of water, calm and tranquil. That is the state of being you are in when everything is in order in your life. Heaven is that place where such order reigns securely forever. Peace is the fruit of being in right relationship with God, and in God, with others. When I am living under the Lordship of Christ, then I know peace. During Mass, we are asked to extend a sign that we long for greater tranquility and greater order in our lives and in the Church. As a gesture of that, we extend our hands as a sign of peace to each other.

At this point, the Mass is also following a biblical principle by asking us to extend a sign of peace to those around us before we approach the altar to receive communion.

> Therefore, if you bring your gift to the altar, and there recall that your brother has anything against you, leave your gift there at the altar, go first and be reconciled with your brother, and then come and offer your gift. (Matthew 5:23–24)

This takes us back to the petition in the Our Father where we pray "Forgive us our trespasses, as we forgive those who trespass against us." We are to be agents of the mercy of God because we ourselves have received His mercy. That sounds nice—until you have to do it. Then, almost nothing in Christianity is harder than forgiving.

We're not talking about excusable faults and foibles, we're talking about forgiving real, nasty, cruel, spiteful, mean, low and unrepentant sinners who knew exactly what they were doing when they hurt us, did it anyway, and never said they were sorry. That's what extending forgiveness is about, and Jesus very deliberately ties our own forgiveness to our willingness to swallow this seemingly bitter pill. He tells us, "When you stand to pray, forgive anyone against whom you have a grievance, so that your heavenly Father may in turn forgive you your transgressions" (Mark 11:25). There is not the faintest suggestion that if we refuse to extend mercy to others, we shall find it for ourselves. That puts us in a desperate bind, because it's impossible for us to do this—unless we rely on His help to enable us. That's one more reason why we need "daily bread," the grace of our Eucharistic Lord who enables us to do the seemingly impossible and forgive people who have sinned against us.

Similarly, if you approach the altar and realize someone has something against you, you are to make peace with him. Notice we are not asked to remember those who have sinned against us, but rather we are to think about those against whom we have sinned. In short, if we are going to be followers of the Prince of Peace, whom we are about to receive in the Eucharist, we must be at peace, to the best of our ability, with *everyone*. The *Sign of Peace* is our attempt to come to peace with all those people in our lives with whom we are not at peace, maybe because of what we've done to them, or because of what they've done to us.

If you approach the *Sign of Peace* like this, you may find yourself thinking of that cousin who owes you money, or your former friend who betrayed your trust and spread all those lies about you, or that girl in grade school that you made fun of all those years ago. The Mass challenges us to make peace with these people before approaching the Lord in communion. But of course, there's a big problem. We can't literally reach out to these people and receive the sign of peace from them. What can we do to be reconciled in such circumstances?

What you can do is see your cousin, your former friend and that grade school girl in those who are actually around you at Mass whose hands you can shake at the *Sign of Peace*. In that gesture of extending your hand and offering peace, you can both extend peace to those people whose hands you actually shake, while also symbolically extending peace to all those in your life with whom you are not at peace. While shaking hands, think about those people in your life you have something against or who have something against you. See their faces on the faces of those whose hands you shake while you say, "Peace be with you." Where it is appropriate, prudent and possible, ask God for the wisdom and grace to make amends to those whom you have hurt. For you must be at peace. We must be able to extend peace to all, if we are to dare to approach Jesus. That requires humility and effort.

But there is also a complexity here. Sometimes we cannot truly offer peace all the way. Sometimes the hurt is so deep, or the conflict so complex, the situation so entangled with sins on both sides that complete reconciliation is really not possible right now. That's okay. If that's where you are, it's enough to say to God, "I'm not sure I truly desire reconciliation right now. But I do desire to desire reconciliation, because that is what you ask of me. I am willing to be made willing to extend a sign of peace. But this is who I am right now. I am going to do what I can right now even if it is not much. I will extend as much peace as I can to those with whom I am not at peace. Today, I cannot shake hands, maybe just one little finger. Hopefully I will one day shake with my whole hand and really mean it, eye to eye, but right now I'm going to do what I can. I'm going to extend the peace that I am able to extend." We intend by this sign of peace our *willingness* to go all the way in extending peace in our broken relationships.

THE LAMB OF GOD

After this, the priest breaks the Host and mingles a small piece with the Blood of Christ as we say or sing:

Lamb of God, You take away the sins of the world. Have mercy on us.

Lamb of God, You take away the sins of the world. Have mercy on us.

Lamb of God, You take away the sins of the world. Grant us peace.

The phrase "Lamb of God" comes from the Gospel of John. John the Baptist identifies Jesus as the Lamb of God (John 1:29). He is linking Jesus to the Passover of Exodus 12 and directing us to look there to understand Jesus' identity. Who is Jesus? He is God's Passover Lamb, the One whose shed blood saves God's family from the Angel of Death.

At the time of Jesus, during the celebration of the Passover, a Jewish family would bring a lamb to the temple to be sacrificed in order to receive forgiveness for their sins. Not coincidentally, John carefully notes that Jesus was crucified at noon on the day of Preparation for Passover. Why? Because at that moment, Passover lambs were being slaughtered in the temple. He is telling us that the Passover is now being fulfilled: God's Lamb is being sacrificed to take away the sins of the family of God, namely the whole world. So when we cry out "Lamb of God," we are saying that Jesus is the One whom God has sent to bring about the forgiveness of the sins of the whole world. Recognizing that, we say, "Have mercy on us." Why? Because His sacrifice also includes me. He died for my sins—*my* sins.

In front of the Supreme Court of the United States there is a statue of Lady Justice. She holds the scales of justice in her hands, and she is blindfolded. Why is Justice blind? In justice, people get what they deserve without prejudice or partiality, regardless of wealth or race or creed. But God's mercy is not like Lady Justice. Mercy is not blind. Mercy sees. From the cross, Jesus sees and says, "Father forgive them for they do not know what they are doing." Jesus' tormentors deserve punishment but they and we are offered forgiveness.

That's not to say mercy and justice are opposites. On the contrary, God's mercy *fulfills* justice. Mercy fulfills justice by overflowing it, in the sense that we do not get what we deserve in our relationship with God. Instead, *Jesus* got what we deserved by dying on our behalf. And because of this, we receive mercy. We receive a fresh start, a new beginning. That's why Paul says, "For our sake he made him to be sin who did not know sin, so that we might become the righteousness of God in him" (2 Corinthians 5:21). The Lamb of God is taking away the sins of the world. He is taking what we deserve. So we are going to cry out "mercy" and we are going to cry out "peace." Because it is through mercy, through this fresh start and this new beginning, that we are going to go from a broken relationship with God to peace, which is the fruit of being in right relationship with God.

IN THE SHOES OF THE CENTURION

After this, the priest elevates the Host and declares, "This is the Lamb of God who takes away the sins of the world. Happy are those who are called to his supper." We reply, "Lord I am not worthy to receive you, but only say the Word and I shall be healed." Where does that reply come from? From Scripture!

When he entered Capernaum, a centurion approached him and appealed to him, saying, "Lord, my servant is lying at home paralyzed, suffering dreadfully." He said to him, "I will come and cure him." The centurion said in reply, "Lord, I am not worthy to have you enter under my roof; only say the Word and my servant will be healed. For I too am a person subject to authority, with soldiers subject to me. And I say to one, 'Go,' and he goes; and to another, 'Come here,' and he comes; and to my slave, 'Do this,' and he does it." When Jesus heard this, he was amazed and said to those following him, "Amen, I say to you, in no one in Israel have I found such faith. I say to you, many will come from the east and the west, and will recline with Abraham, Isaac, and Jacob

at the banquet in the Kingdom of heaven, but the
children of the kingdom will be driven out into the
outer darkness, where there will be wailing and
grinding of teeth." And Jesus said to the centurion,
"You may go; as you have believed, let it be done
for you." And at that very hour (his) servant was
healed. (Matthew 8:5–13)

The Church is inviting us to recognize that Jesus, who
is in fact going to come to dwell in us, has the power to heal
and has the power to set us free. The Church places us in
the shoes of a man whom Jesus did not merely commend:
Jesus was *amazed* at the Centurion. The Centurion was
not even a Jew. But this Gentile had greater faith than
anyone in Israel. Now, by the power of the Holy Spirit in
the Eucharist, we who are likewise unworthy of God can
amaze Christ with our faith!

A lot of us are in that centurion's shoes. We are carrying
around so much pain, not just for ourselves but for those
we love, that all we are doing is trying to manage that
pain. We keep a mask on that says we're doing fine, but
inside we're dying. This is not what Christ wills for us. So
the Church teaches us to say, "Only say the word and my
soul shall be healed." He wants you to be set free from all
that bondage, all that darkness, all that holds you back
on the inside. This same Christ Who responded to the
centurion's faith is the One we meet in Communion. He

is the One who awaits us in this holy moment of shared union. He wants to meet us and change our lives.

TRANSFORMED INTO CHRIST

When you come forward for Communion, do you know what Jesus Christ intends for you through this encounter? Not merely that your life should change, but that it be completely transformed. He intends to encounter you, set you free and transform you into Him! St. Thomas Aquinas teaches that "the proper effect of receiving this sacrament is the transformation of the human being into Jesus Christ." What God did through the hands of the priest and the supernatural power of the Spirit to the bread and wine, He intends to do in a similar way to *you when you receive Communion.* You might wonder if that's true, why don't we see a greater impact on the lives of Catholics who have been going to Mass for decades? Maybe you're thinking that you've been receiving Communion for years and haven't experienced much of a transformation into Jesus Christ. What explains this?

There is a philosophical principle that sheds some light on the question of why such little transformation seems to actually happen to us who go to Communion so frequently. The principle is, *that which is received is received according to the mode of the receiver.* Notice what the principle doesn't say; it doesn't say that the receiver receives according to the will of the giver, but rather, based on the capacity of the receiver to receive. Jesus Christ who approaches us and gives Himself to us as the Eucharist, intends to transform us into Himself. But that doesn't automatically mean we will be transformed into Him. Why? Because what we actually receive in that moment of encounter with Jesus Christ at Communion depends on our capacity to receive what Jesus is ready to give.

WE RECEIVE AS MUCH AS WE EXPECT AND DESERVE

How much of the Lord's transforming power do we receive in Communion? *As much as we expect.* What we expect to receive is connected to how well we have disposed or readied ourselves to receive. Think of it this way. If you thought you were going to receive enough gifts at your birthday party to fill the trunk of your car, what would you do? You'd empty out the trunk so it was ready to receive the gifts. You would be creating the proper "disposition" in the car, by clearing out those things that would get in the way of the gifts.

When it comes to receiving the Lord Jesus Christ in Communion, there is no car trunk large enough to receive all that He is ready to give. Think of your expectant faith as you approach Communion to be like a container being put under a waterfall. No matter the size of the container, the waterfall will fill it to overflowing. If our readiness to receive is the size of a thimble or a small cup, that is all that we will receive. If it is the size of a five gallon bucket, or a fifty gallon drum, we will still be filled to overflowing. Jesus Christ offers a waterfall of sanctifying grace to us at Communion. As we exercise our expectant faith, we are stretching our capacity to receive more and more of Him into us and thus be transformed.

But note that our tradition says that we not only receive as much as we expect, but as much as we *deserve*. On the one hand, we deserve nothing, and could never on our own be worthy of receiving Jesus Christ into our very being. However, He has plunged us into His divine life at Baptism, making us part of His family, and naming us adopted sons and daughters of God. And so we are welcomed at the table to share in the Passover Lamb of God. So what does it mean "to deserve"? It means that we are living according to the call we have received. That's why the Church puts forward the principle that only those in a state of grace are to come forward to Communion. A generation ago, this was clear. Today, not so much.

When it's time to stand up and get in line for Communion, what goes through your mind? Is it what the Lord would expect or deserve? If you are like me, you will be tempted to focus on what's going on around you rather than preparing for the event of receiving Jesus Christ in the Eucharist. "What an ugly shirt that guy is wearing. Oh, look who decided to show up at Mass today. I'm amazed *she* has the gall to receive Communion! I hate this song!" Or maybe you are not thinking anything—a hundred miles away in your thoughts, tuned out in your mind while your body is shuffling up to the front of the line. Why are we so easily distracted from the encounter we are about to have with Jesus Christ? Jesus, who loves you so much, is about to put Himself into your hands at Communion. Do you see how available Christ is to you? He's completely putting Himself into your hands. When you go to receive, then please return the favor. Pray some brief prayer like the following:

> Jesus, I completely place myself at Your disposal at this Communion. All I desire is to welcome You with all the love in my heart. Oh God, stretch me to receive what it is You want to give. Jesus, I say yes to You with all that I am and all that I have. I beg that You would conquer in me all that resists You, and do with me what You will.

Then, as you receive, welcome Him into your very being with reverence, devotion and humility, so that as He dissolves into you, you will be more fully transformed into Him.

GO! YOU ARE SENT!

What is really striking is how quickly Mass ends after Communion. You receive Him, have a moment to commune with Him in song and silence, and then suddenly after the *Closing Prayer* and *Dismissal* you are out the door. It is time to go. The source, summit and center of our faith is now going to be a source of missionary dynamism. That's what the *Dismissal* (in Latin *"Ite missa est"* or "Go! You are sent!") is asking of us. During Mass (which gets its name from this line) we have worshiped God the Father with Christ as our High Priest and Sacrifice. We put ourselves in His hands through the priest's hands. We have received back from Him so much more than we gave. In the Eucharist, we received His very life, the body, blood, soul, and divinity of Jesus Christ.

Now, having had four life-changing encounters with Jesus Christ, we are to go out into the world in the power of His Spirit. At the altar, the priest presided. Now in the world, we lay people preside, using our heart, mind, strength, and gifts to love God and neighbor. We are tasked with nothing less than the work of bringing Christ into every nook and cranny of the whole world. We are, as St. Theresa of Avila said, Christ's hands and feet on earth. Having encountered Jesus we now go out to bring that encounter to others. Jesus Christ, who changes your life when you are open to meet Him, will shine forth through you as go forth to love and serve the Lord.

Thanks be to God!

I WANT TO SEE!

When Mass ended I remained with Jesus
to render Him thanks.
My thirst and hunger do not diminish
after I have received
Him in the Blessed Sacrament, but rather,
increase steadily.
Oh, how sweet was the conversation I
held with Paradise this morning.
The Heart of Jesus and my own, if you
will pardon my expression,
fused. They were no longer two hearts
beating but only one.
My heart disappeared as if it were a drop
in the ocean.

St. Pio of Pietrelcina

In this book we've explored how the Mass is an event involving four encounters with Jesus Christ that have the power to change our lives. Jesus is present and active in the community, in His Word, in the priest and in the Eucharist. We've discovered there is a drama unfolding at Mass, and heard the call to enter it. We've seen that the Mass involves a sacrifice on an altar that is also a table, with a meal that satisfies us and, paradoxically, make us hungry for more.

I don't want to miss an encounter with Jesus ever again. I want to join with those around me and enter the worship of God in Heaven. I want to hear a personal Word for me every time I hear the Readings and Gospel. I deeply desire to be "all in" at every Mass. Most of all, I hunger for Jesus Himself, the Bread of Life, who hungers to feed me with His very body and blood. But how can that happen? What can we do to grow in the attitude of alert readiness for these encounters with Jesus Christ at Mass? We can spend time with Him outside of Mass, especially in Eucharistic Adoration.

EXPOSING THE HEART OF JESUS

What happens at Eucharistic Adoration? Put simply, Jesus Christ in His Eucharistic presence is exposed and adored. The vessel the Church uses to do this is called a monstrance. "Monstrance" comes from the Latin word *monstrare,* which means to show, unveil, disclose or reveal.

What is being unveiled and shown in the monstrance? The presence of Christ; His heart—revealed to us. The Monstrance is often a golden vessel shaped like the sun, with the Eucharist in the center, encircled by golden rays. This conveys two simple meanings: first, like the heat of the sun, Jesus Christ's Eucharistic presence is communicating a love to us that will warm our hearts and even set them on fire. And second, as the sun gives off light, He is shedding light upon us that dispels the darkness and confusion in our minds.

In Eucharistic Adoration, we will experience *monstrarae.* Jesus Christ is there to reveal His Heart to you. As you receive that love, you will feel a tug to share what is in your heart with Him. As He reveals His heart to you, He will also unveil your heart to yourself, and you are invited to unveil your heart to Him. In short, He invites you to go before the Blessed Sacrament and simply say, "Here I am Lord, just the way I am. I open myself to you, Jesus. I welcome Your presence, light and love and I give you my heart."

AT THE FEET OF JESUS

For many people, it won't be easy to just be there in Adoration. We want to be active. We want to do something or read something. We fidget and want to fill the time we have in front of the Blessed Sacrament. The challenge we face is to learn how to sit at His feet and be present to Him. This might seem very strange and foreign at first. You may be thinking, "This isn't doing a lot of good. I'm just sitting here. Nothing's happening. I don't hear anything. I'm distracted, I'm bored, and my eyelids are heavy. I'm not getting anything out of this. I need to be doing something." Those thoughts are not surprising for people who grew up in a world focused on doing. Even if your experience of Adoration began there, trust me when I tell you that it won't end there, unless you just stop going.

Do you remember Mary and Martha, the sisters of Lazarus? They knew that Jesus was coming to visit them. If you want to welcome Jesus into your life, you have two options. You can be like Martha and run around doing hospitable things to show Him that He is welcome. Or, you can be like Mary and sit at the feet of Jesus and gaze into His eyes. What does Jesus say when Martha says, "Lord, do you not care that my sister has left me by myself to do the serving? Tell her to help me." Jesus says, "Martha, Martha, you are anxious and concerned about many things. There is need of only one thing. Mary has chosen the better part and it will not be taken from her" (Luke 10:38–42). In other words, God wants us to be human *beings*, not human *doings*.

UNTIE HIM AND LET HIM GO FREE

Consider the story of Lazarus, whom Jesus raised from the dead. John tells us that when Jesus raised Lazarus, "the dead man came out, tied hand and foot with burial bands, and his face was wrapped in a cloth" (John 11:44). The last thing that Jesus says regarding Lazarus' situation is, "Unbind him and let him go." Jesus is referring to the many small strips of cloth that were securing the main burial cloth that completely covered Lazarus. He could not be untied all at once. He would have regained his mobility a little bit at a time as each strip was removed. The best thing he could do to support this action of being set free was to stand there and be still. Similarly, we are invited to sit and be still in the presence of the Lord in Eucharistic Adoration. Like Lazarus we give the Lord a chance to unbind us and let us go free.

God gives us new life, but that new life doesn't instantly make us perfect. In Adoration, God sets us free with His light and love, removing one strip at a time. The loving gaze of the Lord and warmth of His presence gently sets us free. We have to grow, to overcome our limitations and to learn to see, walk and serve. How does this take place? The answer is: by beginning at His feet, simply saying, "Jesus, in your love, unbind me and let me go free." If you do this, you will find that little by little, one strip at a time, you will be freed to live the new life that was given you in Baptism. You will begin to experience a new level of joy, peace and freedom, and come to know more deeply, the joy that Jesus takes in you. You will begin to see the effects of just being in the presence of the Son and opening yourself to His presence. Sort of like getting a suntan. Just sitting there exposed to the Son is all you need to do to have the Son impact your life.

Consider the following quote from Hans Urs von Balthasar; while not originally referencing Adoration, his words apply to the powerful effect of placing yourself before the gaze of the Lord Jesus in Eucharistic Adoration:

> Holiness consists in enduring God's glance. It may appear mere passivity to withstand the look of an eye; but everyone knows how much exertion is required when this occurs in an essential encounter. Our glances mostly brush past each other indirectly, or they turn quickly away, or they give themselves not personally, but only socially. So too do we constantly flee from God into a distance that is theoretical, rhetorical, sentimental, aesthetic, or most frequently pious. Or we flee from Him to external works. And yet, the best thing would be to surrender one's naked heart to the fire of this all-penetrating glance. The heart would then itself have to catch fire if it were not always artificially dispersing the rays that come to it as through a magnifying glass. Such enduring would

be the opposite of a Stoic's hardening his face: it would be yielding, declaring oneself beaten, capitulating, entrusting oneself, casting oneself into him. It would be childlike loving, since for children the glance of the Father is not painful: with wide-open eyes, they look into his. Thérèse—great little Thérèse—could do it. Augustine's magnificent formula on the essence of eternity: *videntem videre*—"to look at him who is looking at you."[2]

Do you really want to be transformed? Do you really want to go to Mass and have four encounters with Jesus that change your life? Then take time to be with Him *outside* of Mass. Ask Christ to set *you* on fire and then let His gaze rest on you until you feel your heart burning within you, as the disciples did who walked with Jesus on the road to Emmaus. Then you will burn with the desire to go Mass, because you will know that He awaits you there. Jesus waits for you. To meet you. In the community. In His Word. In the priest. In the Eucharist. To change your life.

---

2. *The Grain of Wheat,* Hans Urs von Balthasar, 1995, Ignatius Press, San Francisco, 3–4.

THE MASS:

Four Encounters with Jesus that will Change Your Life

By Dr. Tom Curran

INTRODUCTION: Is Mass Boring or are We?

1. The book begins with a quote by Pope Benedict XVI. Can you think of an event or an encounter with a person that has given your life a new direction and new meaning? What about your experience of Jesus Christ? Would you consider your relationship with Jesus to be decisive for your life? How?

2. In the *Introduction*, Dr. Curran talks about being a participant rather than a spectator at Mass. At what point in the Mass do find it easiest to be "in the game"? When is it easy to get distracted and feel like you're "in the stands"?

3. Tom emphasizes that the Mass is not only a ritual but an event. Every day we enact rituals—like shaking hands in greeting—that don't feel much like a special event, because they are repeated so often. What sacrament do you most easily see as an event (e.g. Baptism, Holy Matrimony, etc.)? Why?

4. What are the four ways that Jesus Christ is present at Mass? Which of these four "presences" of Jesus has been the most significant in your life? How?

CHAPTER ONE: I Once was Blind, but Now I See

1. What part of the story about the widow and the friend at the funeral touched you the most? Tom quotes Jesus' saying about having eyes and not seeing, and ears and not hearing. Can you relate that to your experience of Mass?

2. Dr. Curran explains a principle in theology "The quality of your recognition is made manifest by your response" by telling the story of watching the football game with his wife. Can you remember a time when your response to a situation showed a lack of recognizing what was really happening? What about at Mass? What part of the Mass do you have the most difficulty understanding? How does that impact your "response" at that moment?

3. In the book, we are asked if we have ever found ourselves bored at Mass. Have you had that experience? If so, what would you identify as the source of your boredom? What does Dr. Curran identify as possible sources of our boredom? His conclusion is that if we are bored at Mass, we have missed the encounter with Jesus Christ. Does that make sense to you? Why or why not?

4. Dr. Curran explores three reasons he didn't see or hear clearly at Mass. What are those reasons? Can you relate to the three reasons outlined? In what way?

5. What does the word "Eucharist" mean? Why do you go to Mass? Do you ever feel a need to thank God for all He has given you? When does that show up in your life? What do you do about it?

CHAPTER TWO: Jesus Christ Present in the Community

1. Dr. Curran tells the story of driving home and seeing his kids "on the lookout." How does that shed light on how we are to be present at Mass?

2. The book explores the attitudes of those present at Mass as uninterested spectators or critical observers. Have you ever fallen into these attitudes? At which point(s) during the Mass? What do you do about it?

3. The first encounter with Jesus Christ that the book draws attention to is Jesus Christ's presence in the Community. Were you aware how extensive the Community gathered at Mass is? What clues does your church building give you as to who is included in the community gathered at Mass?

4. At Mass, Heaven breaks into earth, and earth is drawn up into Heaven. What helps you foster a lively awareness of this truth? When you first realized that at Mass you are brought before the throne of God the Father, together with angels and saints and Jesus Christ Himself, what happened?

CHAPTER THREE: Jesus Christ Present in the Word

1. The book explores the reasons behind standing and sitting at different parts of the Mass. What would it mean for you to try to sit during the Readings the way Mary of Bethany sat at the feet of Jesus?

2. In the Readings, we encounter Jesus Christ as the Word, as One Who has a message for each of us. Can you remember a Mass when God communicated the message you most needed to hear? What happened?

3. Do you have a Bible? What part does it play in your relationship with God? Have you related to the Bible as merely a book to be studied, or as an Owner's Manual for living a godly life? What benefits did that bring to your life?

4. Dr. Curran describes a third way to relate to the Bible—as a place of encounter. Have you ever approached the Bible as the Word of God that is "living" and "active"? Why do you think some Catholics seem to have little or no expectations that God will communicate a message just for them during the Liturgy of the Word? What can we do to increase those expectations?

5. In the Prayers of the Faithful, we on earth are drawn into the intercessory prayer of Jesus Christ and the saints in Heaven. Why do so many people get the concept of intercessory prayer backwards (page 66)? Have you ever experienced intercessory prayer in the way Tom describes? What happened?

CHAPTER FOUR: Jesus Christ Present in the Priest

1. Chapter Four begins with a story about a group of seminarians watching a movie, and the line, "There is something about the cross that a Catholic should not want to escape." What would it mean for your life if you were able to live your daily activities in light of the Cross of Christ?

2. At Mass, the Paschal Mystery breaks into our present moment. What does the word "memory" mean in the Jewish tradition? Did you come to a new or deeper understanding of the special presence of Jesus Christ in the priest? What did you learn?

3. The Presentation of the Gifts is described as a dramatic part of the Mass for the congregation. What struck you about the idea of offering yourself as a spiritual sacrifice? Have you ever gone "all in" the way Dr. Curran describes during this part of the Mass?

4. When the water is poured into the wine, the priest prays that our humanity will be mixed with the divinity of Christ. What does that say about the importance of what happens at Mass? Does the awareness of your sharing in Christ's divine nature impact how you see yourself and others? How?

5. Christ's presence in the priest is most profoundly expressed in the Epiclesis and the Prayer of Consecration. What is the "Epiclesis"? Why does God work through the priest, and not just the Holy Spirit, to change the bread and wine into the body and blood of Christ? What does this part of the Mass teach us about the way we fulfill our God given mission on earth?

6. At Mass, we do not merely recall Christ's Passion, death and Resurrection; this reality is made present and effective for us today. What implication does the Church draw out of this regarding the way in which our sinful actions today affect what Jesus suffered 2,000 years ago? How might an awareness of this change our actions and decisions each and every day?

CHAPTER FIVE: Jesus Christ Present in the Eucharist

1. What struck you about Tom's description of serving the Easter Vigil Mass with Pope John Paul II? How did he contrast that with the typical, daily Mass? Why does Tom conclude that there is no such a thing as an "ordinary" Mass?

2. Why does Christ's presence in the Eucharist bring the dimension of the future into our present at Mass? How might this future-oriented aspect of the Mass help us live here, now and today?

3. The Lord's Prayer is called the perfect prayer because it was taught by Jesus Himself. What in the Lord's Prayer indicates that we are still "on the way"— we have not yet arrived at our heavenly home? Why do we pray the Lord's Prayer right before Communion?

4. What significance do you see in the Sign of Peace? What did you think about Dr. Curran's suggestion that the Sign of Peace be an opportunity to extend peace to all those with whom you are not at peace? Does anyone come to mind?

5. Where does our response, "Lord I am not worthy to receive you, but only say the word and I shall be healed" come from? Why was Jesus "amazed" at the faith of the Centurion, and what does that have to do with us? How can we put ourselves in the place of the Centurion when we prepare for Communion?

6. What does St. Thomas Aquinas teach is the "proper effect" of receiving Holy Communion? Can you remember a time when you felt deeply transformed when you received Communion? What do you think holds us back from experiencing a personal encounter with Jesus in Holy Communion?

7. Dr. Curran refers to a principle of sacramental theology: "That which is received is received according to the mode of the receiver" (For example, a cup will receive what is poured into it based on its size and shape.) Have you ever considered that Jesus Christ desires to "pour into" you more than you are able to receive at Communion? What does that make you want to do?

AFTERWORD: I Want to See!

1. Where in your life do you encounter Jesus Christ outside of Mass? Does this help increase your awareness of Him at Mass? In what ways?

2. What is your experience of Eucharistic Adoration? What is the purpose of designing a Monstrance to be shaped like the sun? What other shapes for a Monstrance have you seen (e.g. a church)? Was that shape meaningful or helpful in your time of adoration? How?

3. In Eucharistic Adoration, Jesus Christ intends to unveil His heart to you, and invites you to unveil your heart to Him. Have you ever experienced that? What makes that easy and what makes that difficult?

4. Discuss the quote from Fr. von Balthasar about "enduring God's glance." Why would enduring God's glance be difficult? Why would it transform?

5. As a result of reading this book, what will you do to participate more fully at Mass? What were the most insightful or helpful parts of the book?

To order the book:
The Mass: Four Encounters with Jesus that will Change Your Life

Or other presentations by Dr. Tom Curran
on how to grow in your appreciation, understanding and living out
of your Catholic faith, available on CD, DVD or MP3.

Please call toll free **1-888-765-9269**
or go to **www.MyCatholicFaith.org**